TRAILS WEST

Prepared by the
Special Publications Division

National Geographic Society
Washington, D. C.

TRAILS WEST

Contributing Authors: MARC SIMMONS, WALLACE
STEGNER, CHARLES MCCARRY, ROBERT LAXALT, DON
DEDERA, LOUIS DE LA HABA

Contributing Photographers: DAVID HISER, LOWELL
GEORGIA, MELINDA BERGE, JONATHAN T. WRIGHT, KERBY
SMITH, TONY O'BRIEN, JIM BRANDENBURG, GORDON
BEALL, R. STEVEN FULLER

Published by
The National Geographic Society
ROBERT E. DOYLE, *President*
MELVIN M. PAYNE, *Chairman of the Board*
GILBERT M. GROSVENOR, *Editor*
MELVILLE BELL GROSVENOR, *Editor Emeritus*

Prepared by
The Special Publications Division
ROBERT L. BREEDEN, *Editor*
DONALD J. CRUMP, *Associate Editor*
PHILIP B. SILCOTT, *Senior Editor*
MERRILL WINDSOR, *Managing Editor*
CAROL A. ENQUIST, STEPHEN J. HUBBARD, TEE LOFTIN,
    LUIS TORRES, *Research*

Illustrations and Design
JOHN AGNONE, *Picture Editor*
SUEZ KEHL, *Art Director*
JODY BOLT, *Consulting Art Director*
TURNER HOUSTON, CINDA ROSE, *Design Assistants*
LOUIS DE LA HABA, BARBARA GRAZZINI, STEPHEN
    J. HUBBARD, JENNIFER C. URQUHART, SUZANNE
    VENINO, *Picture Legends*
JOHN D. GARST, JR., CHARLES W. BERRY, GEORGE
    E. COSTANTINO, MARGARET DEANE GRAY, ALFRED
    L. ZEBARTH, *Map Research, Design, and Production*

Production and Printing
ROBERT W. MESSER, *Production Manager*
GEORGE V. WHITE, *Assistant Production Manager*
RAJA D. MURSHED, JUNE L. GRAHAM, CHRISTINE A.
    ROBERTS, DAVID V. SHOWERS, *Production Assistants*

DEBRA A. ANTONINI, BARBARA BRICKS, JANE H. BUXTON,
    KAY DASCALAKIS, ROSAMUND GARNER, SUZANNE
    J. JACOBSON, AMY E. METCALFE, CLEO PETROFF,
    KATHERYN M. SLOCUM, SUZANNE VENINO, *Staff
    Assistants*

ANNE K. MCCAIN, *Index*

*Distinct in the dawn light, the 135-year-old trace of the
Oregon Trail snakes along a windswept ridge above
Ash Hollow, Nebraska. Pages 2-3: Wagon master Mel
Heaton harnesses an Appaloosa on the Mormon
Honeymoon Trail. Page 1: California-bound emigrants
find themselves in desperate trouble, with an ox "lain
down in its yoke to die." Endpapers: Reenacting a
journey on the Oregon Trail, a 20th-century wagon
train halts for the night near Chimney Rock, Nebraska.
Hardcover design: Straining against ropes, pioneers
try to aid their oxen over a rugged mountain passage.*

PAGES 2-3: MELINDA BERGE; PAGE 1: "CROSSING THE PLAINS" BY CHARLES C. NAHL,
CIRCA 1856, STANFORD UNIVERSITY MUSEUM OF ART, GIFT OF JANE L. STANFORD; END-
PAPERS: DAVID HISER; HARDCOVER: FROM MELINDA BERGE PHOTOGRAPH OF BAS-RELIEF
PANEL BY MAHONRI M. YOUNG, "THIS IS THE PLACE" MONUMENT, SALT LAKE CITY.

DAVID HISER

Foreword

We Americans have a long-standing love affair with the trails that led our westering ancestors toward the sunset. We have read about them in hundreds of books since Francis Parkman's *The Oregon Trail* appeared in the 1840's; we have glorified them in such classic films as *The Covered Wagon;* we have elevated television series like "Wagon Train" to the highest ratings. "Highways of conquest," we dubbed them, as we linked those rude tracks to the migrations that won the continent.

I felt their lure some 30 years ago when I drove westward from Chicago for my first look at the Far West. That land was not exactly unknown to me; I had been reading and teaching and writing about the West for 20 years in eastern and midwestern colleges, but not until a textbook in frontier history paid me a few royalties could I afford such a journey.

What an eye-opening adventure that was! I zigzagged back and forth across the Rockies a dozen times, following one trail after another, stopping now and then to explore the ruins of Fort Bridger, climb Independence Rock to trace the names of pioneers carved there, or thrill at the sight of the ruts of the wagon trains in Oregon's Blue Mountains.

Now and then I asked myself why I was so fascinated by the trails I was following. I knew that, for some time, the number of people they carried was small. Between 1840 and the California gold rush, fewer than 20,000 men, women, and children followed those roads westward—a handful compared with the hordes then flooding the Mississippi Valley, or the hundreds of thousands crossing the Atlantic to seek a better life in the New World. Yet the story of the overland trails was told a thousand times for every one telling of the peopling of the Midwest. Why?

Excitement was there, of course: Indian attacks and desert hardship and even cannibalism. But I suspected that the greatest appeal of the trails lay in the role they played as avenues of progress for the enterprising. The men and women who followed them exemplified—and exaggerated—the hopes and dreams of all Americans for a better life. These were no cautious stay-at-homes content to endure fate's buffeting. They were bold adventurers, willing to risk everything to better themselves economically and socially. They were heeding Horace Greeley's advice—not just to "Go west, young man"—but to "Go west, young man, and grow up with the country!" The roads that the pioneers followed symbolized the spirit of enterprise that sustained the American dream.

Today that spirit flames less strongly in America, but the appeal of the trails has not diminished. As I read and admired the pages that follow in this superb book, I realized why. They tell of high adventure, but they tell also of the hopes and sacrifices that made our nation great. Six writers mirror that spirit as they describe their own experiences in retracing the trails today, and the hardships of the pioneers who preceded them. Talented photographers add their contemporary work to an absorbing selection of historical illustrations. This is a book that not only excites and entertains, but also helps us renew our faith in the West that was, and that lives still in our national spirit.

RAY ALLEN BILLINGTON
The Huntington Library
San Marino, California

Land of the big sky: Day's end sets clouds aflame above the wandering

JONATHAN T. WRIGHT

course of the Bighorn River in southern Montana.

Contents

Highway of Commerce

By Marc Simmons

“The charioteer, as he smacks his whip, feels a bounding elasticity of soul within him . . . impossible to restrain;—even the mules prick up their ears with a peculiarly conceited air, as if in anticipation of that change of scene which will presently follow.”

The place was not Rome but Independence, Missouri; the writer was no classical scholar but a traveler on the American prairies, Josiah Gregg. The year was 1831, and Gregg was about to set out, in a train of a hundred freight wagons crammed to the tops of their sideboards with merchandise, for distant Santa Fe.

The teamster—Gregg's charioteer—had been hired somewhere in the Missouri settlements for a wage of $20 a month. For that sum he was expected to drive his fractious mules by day, pull his wagon into position at evening to form part of a defensive circle, stand a turn at night guard, and put up with thirst, sandstorms, rattlesnakes, mosquitoes, and scalp-raising Indians.

Late one midsummer's day, at the opposite end of the road of Gregg's adventure, I reflected upon the men of durable spirit who, in spite of looming hardships, could experience an expansion of soul at the prospect of a trip over the Santa Fe Trail. I was standing on the brow of a low hill overlooking New Mexico's ancient capital, near the spot where drivers of the wagon caravans caught their first glimpse of journey's end.

Far to the west, fanlike rays of the sloping sun tinged piles of oceanic clouds with shades of red and purple. Behind Santa Fe, in its darkening cup of a valley, rose the soaring ramparts of the Sangre de

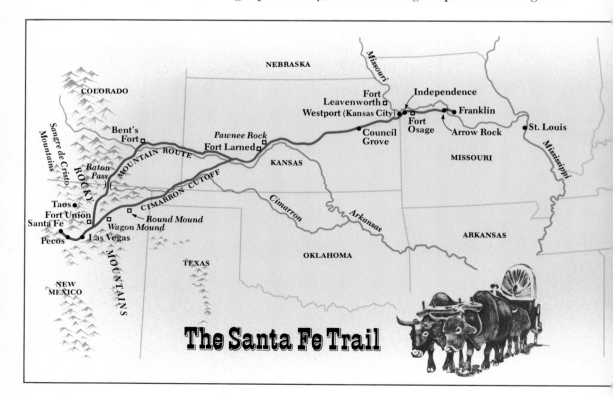

The Santa Fe Trail

Cristo Mountains. Earlier a passing shower had scrubbed them clean, so that now, catching the refracted beams of fading sunlight, they shone like glass. The rainfall had also liberated the perfume of ponderosa and piñon pine. The scented air, drifting down from the higher peaks, was as familiar to me as the adobe buildings and narrow streets of old Santa Fe.

From half a lifetime in New Mexico, I could understand the enthusiasm of men like Gregg's teamsters. On the surface, at least, they were drawn west by economic motives—the chance to turn a dollar in the southwestern trade. But perhaps unconsciously they also responded to the challenge of a stirring, spartan life on the trail, and even more to the spell cast by Santa Fe in its storybook setting. There in the gloaming, I felt keenly a sense of kinship with those long-ago travelers who had paused, just as I did now, to breathe deeply and look and marvel.

One of the best known of that pioneering breed was Josiah Gregg himself. He joined his first caravan not as a teamster but as a health-seeker. Well educated but physically weak, he hoped that the western air and regular exercise would cure his various ailments. Although, he informs us, he commenced the journey as a semi-invalid riding in a carriage, "Before the close of the first week, I saddled my pony. And when we reached the buffalo range, I was not only as eager for the chase as the sturdiest of my companions, but I enjoyed far more exquisitely my share of the buffalo meat than all the delicacies which were ever devised to provoke the most fastidious appetite."

Josiah Gregg found both a remedy for ill health and a new vocation. The Santa Fe Trail claimed him, as it did so many others. Eight times he crossed and recrossed the plains as a merchant before settling down with quill and ink to capture on paper a fleeting era. His *Commerce of the Prairies*, first printed in 1844, remains the classic account of trail life and customs.

The main story of the Santa Fe Trail is neatly marked off at the beginning and end: The trail endured for a scant 60 years, from its opening in 1821 until 1880, when completion of the railroad to Santa Fe put it out of business. But another chapter has been added to the saga during the present century. People with a variety of motives and modes of travel—foot, horseback, wagon, or automobile—have been moved to retrace the old route. For them the spirit of the Santa Fe traders is somehow recaptured at the river crossings and watering holes, beneath the shadows of landmark mountains, in the quiet ruins of forts, and at those rare spots where, however faintly, caravan tracks are indelibly engraved in the earth.

On a steamy August morning I began my own journey over the Santa Fe Trail. In New Franklin, Missouri, I discovered that a plain granite marker sits squarely in the middle of the placid little town's main street. Its chiseled inscription reads: "Franklin, 'Cradle of the Santa Fe Trail.' This trail, one of the great highways of the world, stretched nearly one thousand miles from Franklin, Missouri, to Santa Fe, New Mexico. 'From Civilization to Sundown.'"

Among America's chief pathways of   *(Continued on page 16)*

Reaching from Missouri to New Mexico—more than 900 miles—the Santa Fe Trail cut across prairie, mountain, and desert. Travelers had a choice of two branches: The northern angled through the Colorado Rockies, a difficult passage for wagons; the southern, or Cimarron cutoff, shortened the journey by a hundred miles but took travelers far from reliable sources of water.

Salute to tradition at Independence

Independence, Missouri—once the principal departure point for westbound travelers on the Santa Fe, Oregon, and California trails—commemorates the past at an annual September festival in Courthouse Square. Emigrants gathered here in early spring to buy supplies, outfit wagons, and select teams of oxen or mules before starting the long trek west. In the pioneer tradition, Carl Smart breaks a yoke of oxen to harness in Missouri Town 1855, a recreated frontier village near Independence. Many wagoners preferred oxen over mules or horses because of their greater strength and endurance. In the village's blacksmith shop, Smart welds a hinge for a wagon toolbox.

By moonlight, roustabouts unload a steamboat from St. Louis at Wayne City Landing on the Missouri River. Wagons haul the cargo

*up the steep hill to nearby Independence, for repacking on large
overland freight wagons heading westward on the Santa Fe Trail.*

Harsh reality of the trail: Two Sisters of Loretto kneel at the grave of a companion who has died of cholera on the way to Santa Fe in 1867. The dread disease claimed more lives on the emigrant roads than all the Indian attacks combined.

westward expansion, the Santa Fe Trail was the oldest, and the first over which wagons were used. It served primarily as a commercial route, traveled by swarms of eager merchants and freighters. But the trail also accommodated mountain men, military expeditions, California-bound emigrants, and a sprinkling of early-day tourists. Taken all together, their experiences form an epic history.

While I was copying down the inscription on the Franklin marker, a friendly farmer in bib overalls came up. "Saw you standing in the street," he said. "I've been here all my life, and I've never gotten around to reading this stone. Thought I ought to take a look."

We talked awhile, and he remarked, "When I was a boy, old-timers claimed that the first Santa Fe traders marked the trail by bending down branches of saplings. You can still see some of our oldest trees, left over from that time, with limbs bent toward the ground

at a right angle." If true, here was a fragment of trail lore that had escaped the notice of formal historians.

The birthplace of the Santa Fe Trail was actually several miles south of the marker where the farmer and I stood that 90-degree morning. Old Franklin, from which the inaugural trading expedition to New Mexico left in 1821, had been improvidently placed on the floodplain of the fickle Missouri River. By 1828 the engulfing waters of the Big Muddy had chased the residents of the community to higher ground and caused the founding of New Franklin.

The man who put Franklin on the historical map and won the appellation "father of the Santa Fe Trail" was William Becknell. Of his early life, we know only that he was a veteran of the War of 1812 who later attained a reputation as an Indian fighter.

When he set out from Franklin in the summer of 1821 with several companions and a string of pack mules loaded with trade goods, Becknell could hardly have guessed that he was riding straight into the history books. Ahead of him lay a vast wilderness, unspoiled and deceptively serene, where buffalo, deer, and pronghorn antelope abounded, and the roving Indians hunted and raided one another unfettered. At the far edge of the plains waited the 200-year-old Spanish colonial city of Santa Fe, home of aristocratic dons and their flashing-eyed ladies.

Santa Fe had held a special appeal for Americans since 1st Lt. Zebulon Pike visited there in 1806. Sent with a small expedition to explore the southwest corner of America's new Louisiana Purchase, Pike strayed into Spanish territory.

Such incursions were strictly forbidden. Spain preferred to keep her imperial borders closed to foreigners. She wanted no revolutionary ideas seeping in from the Eastern Seaboard. Nor would she tolerate any breach in her tight monopoly of colonial trade.

Lieutenant Pike was arrested and detained in Santa Fe long enough to observe the effect of such stern policies upon the residents of this outpost of New Spain. Virtually sealed off from the outside world, they had almost no knowledge of the bumptious young nation to the east. They were forced to conduct their commerce at markets deep in Mexico, where manufactured goods were scarce and costly. Pike was incredulous at the prices common imported cloth and simple articles of hardware brought in Santa Fe.

Such news, carried home by Pike and his men, fired the blood of Yankee merchants. Within the next few years several parties left the Mississippi Valley hoping to pierce the iron wall of Spain's commercial barriers. One of these was a trading expedition organized by James Baird and Robert McKnight, which set out for Santa Fe in April 1812. But their enterprise came to nothing. Royal officials pounced on the traders at Taos, confiscated their wares for public auction, and tossed all ten of the unfortunate men into lice-infested jails. Not until 1820 were they finally released.

Thus William Becknell was not the first entrepreneur to strike for Santa Fe, but his timing was better than his predecessors'. In

Trading post on the Arkansas

Dressed in buckskin and fur, members of the South Platte Free Trappers, a club of history enthusiasts, examine dried chili peppers at Bent's Old Fort in southeastern Colorado. Completed in 1834, the post dominated the fur trade in the southern Rockies for 15 years. Trappers, Indians, and traders met within its walls, which also sheltered weary travelers of the Santa Fe Trail. Below, a television camera operator focuses on the history group. The reconstructed fort, now a national historic site, overlooks a wagon ford on the muddy Arkansas River.

1821 Mexico broke free from Spain, and as an independent nation hastily dismantled the obstacles to foreign commerce.

In Santa Fe Becknell found Governor Facundo Melgares all smiles. Men and women pushed into the crowded plaza, eager to bid for Becknell's merchandise. The demand was tremendous, the canny trader realized. But to try to satisfy it and reap the profits, trains of pack mules would not suffice. Wagons would be needed.

On the journey west, Becknell had angled across the future state of Kansas to the great bend of the Arkansas River. Following that stream into southeastern Colorado, he had prodded and coaxed his mules over the rocky summit of Raton Pass and dropped onto the sandy plains beyond, which extended to the first New Mexico settlements. That route, as he well knew, was a poor one for wagon traffic.

Returning to Missouri, he determined to blaze a wagon road on his next trip. Accordingly he set out the following year from the village of Arrow Rock, just upstream from Franklin, with about 30 men and three wagons. To avoid the mountains and steer as directly as possible for Santa Fe, he left the Arkansas River and headed across the arid plains for the Cimarron.

It was a near-fatal decision. With their water gone, the party wandered for days in search of the Cimarron River, and would likely have missed it entirely but for the good fortune of coming upon a contented bison fresh from the stream. Having survived and mapped the ground, the party established for those to follow a wagon route known as the Cimarron cutoff.

"Quite roomy," Susan Magoffin (above) cheerfully described the sparsely furnished chamber at Bent's Fort where she stayed briefly with her trader husband. In the reconstructed room, guide Kittie MacDonald reads Susan's account of her trip to Santa Fe in 1846—probably the first such journey by an American woman. William Bent (below) built the post with two partners.

A pioneer resident of Arrow Rock who watched Becknell's second expedition return recalled in later years: "When the rawhide thongs of the saddlebags were cut, the Spanish dollars rolled into the gutters, causing great excitement."

The excitement was justified. At that moment Missouri's frontier economy showed signs of faltering. Banks had failed, paper money was unreliable, and coin was scarce. The prospect of a lucrative new trade with Santa Fe and the Mexican provinces beyond seemed like a Heaven-sent opportunity. Becknell had shown the way. Other merchant-adventurers began to lay plans, stock goods, buy wagons, round up oxen or mule teams. From its modest beginning the Santa Fe trade ballooned eventually into a million-dollar-a-year business.

As I drove the 90 miles or so from Franklin westward to Independence, I recalled that the early wagoners brought back more than silver coin. Some of their gingham, mirrors, and needles went for mules and burros, which they drove home in large herds behind the caravans. The jacks among the sturdy Mexican donkeys became the seed-stock sires of the renowned Missouri mules of a future day.

In Independence, historian Bill Goff introduced me to archivist Polly Fowler, a sprightly lady who has spent most of her life delving into the past. With these two experts as guides, I sought out the few remaining local places not buried by metropolitan growth that would be familiar to the men who followed in Becknell's footsteps.

We began our tour at nearby Fort Osage, restored in 1962. The

post is perched on a grassy, timber-fringed bluff above the Missouri River. "The jump-off for the Santa Fe Trail skipped west as the Missouri frontier expanded," Polly explained. "It was Franklin in 1821 and '22, Arrow Rock in '23. In 1824 and 1825, supplies boated upstream from St. Louis were landed here at Fort Osage. Then the point of departure gradually changed to Independence."

The fort has a secure place in trail history; so, too, does George C. Sibley, who served there briefly as a government trader. In 1825 he became one of three commissioners empowered by Congress to undertake an official survey of the Santa Fe Trail.

The project was sponsored by Missouri's ambitious, craggy-jawed Senator Thomas Hart Benton. He saw with great clarity that his state's future was tied to its position as the gateway to the West. By his eloquence he convinced his fellow senators that the United States government should take a hand in nourishing and protecting the swelling flow of traffic over the Santa Fe Trail. Benton's rhetoric also encouraged the expansionists rallying around the slogan and concept of "manifest destiny," embodying the notion that America had a divine mission to extend its boundaries to the Pacific.

Senator Benton won passage of a bill authorizing a survey of the trail and providing a federal appropriation to buy a right-of-way from the Indians. Commissioner Sibley took the initiative in organizing a party to carry out the assignment, and maintained the official journal.

As it turned out, his strenuous efforts bore little fruit. The commission's surveyor mapped the road and some earth mounds were erected to serve as markers (they quickly weathered away). But the expedition unwisely made Taos its destination, instead of Santa Fe; and Taos lay locked in a valley behind the southern Rockies, practically inaccessible by wagon. Sibley's route, so carefully charted, was all but ignored by the masters of the Missouri caravans that followed.

Commissioner Sibley did manage a minor success in his dealings with the Indians. By the main ford of the Neosho River, at a spot that became known as Council Grove, he negotiated a peace treaty with the Osage tribe. A second accord was reached with the Kansas, or Kaw, Indians farther west on Dry Turkey Creek. Neither tribe, however, had ever seriously menaced the Santa Fe trade. The marauding Comanche, Kiowa, Cheyenne, Arapaho, and Apache warriors who spread terror along the far end of the trail were left for the Army to deal with in future years.

In 1827, the year Fort Osage was abandoned, Fort Leavenworth was established farther up the Missouri River to provide military patrols for the Santa Fe and later the Oregon Trail.

At the same time, the town of Independence was born, about three miles from the river, at a site blessed with abundant pasture and watered by sweet-flowing springs. For the next decade and a half, during the cresting of the Santa Fe trade and the beginning of the Oregon migration, Independence was the bright star in the western firmament. To it were drawn all those who craved adventure and reward in the wide lands beyond sundown.

Denver-bound wagon train overtakes a truck-camper stalled in Raton Pass on the New Mexico border. The wagon train, sponsored by the youth agency VisionQuest, found the pass easier going than did Susan Magoffin's party. She wrote: "We came to camp . . . having accomplished the great travel of six or eight hundred yards during the day."

In Independence Square, a picturesque army of traders, trappers, bullwhackers, muleskinners, Mexican herders, and French *voyageurs* gathered each spring as the snow thawed from the trails, and the prairie showed the first hints of green. Lumbering wagons, usually pulled by a dozen mules or six yoke of oxen, were drawn up on the square to be piled with boxes and burlap-wrapped bales. Matthew Field, a New Orleans newspaper reporter who was on hand in 1839, described the scene.

"Every window sash is raised, and anxious faces appear watching with interest the departure," he wrote. "The drivers snap their long whips and swear at their unruly mules, bidding goodby in parentheses between the oaths, to old friends on each side of the street. . . ."

The afternoon that Polly Fowler, Bill Goff, and I strolled around Independence Square, the tempo of activity provided by a few tourists and unhurried shoppers was a far cry from the commotion of days gone by. But though the ground now bears no resemblance to the place Santa Fe traders knew, one still expects somehow to hear the faint rattle of trace chains and the echo of lowing oxen.

FOLLOWING PAGES:
Dead volcano called Round Mound rises alongside the Cimarron cutoff in northeastern New Mexico. Wayfarers used to climb the 800-foot cone for a view reaching to the distant Rockies.
LOWELL GEORGIA

One uncommon traveler who knew those sounds well was a frail slip of a girl named Susan Shelby Magoffin. Born into a wealthy Kentucky family and reared in luxury, Susan went to Santa Fe in 1846 as the bride of veteran trader Samuel Magoffin, a man 27 years her senior. If the commercial excursion was intended to double as a honeymoon, it proved a trying and perilous one for the 18-year-old Susan. Rolling out of Independence in a plush Rockaway carriage provided by her husband, she exclaimed with girlish enthusiasm, "Now the Prairie life begins!" The full record of the hardships she underwent is recounted in her published diary, which has earned a place among the classics of frontier literature.

Even as Susan Magoffin was leaving on her western adventure, Independence had begun to decline as the principal trailhead. Its main steamboat landing on the Missouri was washed away by high water in 1844. Business shifted upstream, slowly at first, to the community of Westport within what is now Kansas City.

In the Flint Hills 150 miles west of Kansas City, I pulled up at Council Grove. Some historians rank the grove with Independence and Santa Fe as one of the three most important places on the trail. For one thing, it offered a bountiful stand of timber—oak, walnut, ash, elm, and hickory. In the miles ahead only occasional cottonwoods grew. So each teamster here cut an extra axletree, wagon pole, or oxbow and stowed it away for emergency use.

Moreover, caravans traditionally completed their organization in the ample shade of the grove. In open balloting, every man helped elect a captain and other officers. Strict, military-like rules prevailed beyond this point, for Council Grove marked the edge of hostile Indian country. Most large wagon trains dragged along at least one small cannon on its carriage, hoping to overawe the red men.

About midway between Council Grove and the Arkansas River, the freighters had to ford Cottonwood Creek. Camping there, they usually parked their wagons in a line across the neck of a looping bow in the stream, thus forming a natural corral for their animals.

I asked directions to the Cottonwood ford at the only cafe in the small town of Durham, Kansas. "Drive west a mile and see Claude Unruh," the genial proprietor advised. "He's been plowing up trail relics for years."

Unruh, his hair faded gray by age and sun, was seated behind a pile of watermelons on the lawn of his farmhouse. A sign advertised them at 7 cents a pound. "You want to know about the ford? Take a look yonder," he said, gesturing toward an open meadow across the road. Ruts of the trail—grassy trenches several inches deep—swept down to a line of trees at the edge of the creek. "The trail crosses right there. On the other side it disappears in a soybean field. Come on. I've got a little museum in my basement."

"What about the watermelons?" I asked with some concern.

"Oh, don't worry about them. They'll sell themselves," and he pointed to a notice written on a metal cash box. It advised customers to weigh a melon and make their own change.

My host's collection included pieces of spurs, wagon parts, a buffalo skull, and an 1835 half-dime. But what caught my attention was a small religious medal of the kind once worn by most of the native population of New Mexico. Though the piece was tarnished, the raised letters could still be read: *Mater Dolorosa,* Our Lady of Sorrows. For me it served as a reminder of a little-known chapter in the annals of the Santa Fe Trail.

Men of Missouri, as historians are fond of telling us, opened the commerce of the trail. But what writers seldom mention is that before long an active corps of New Mexico merchants joined in. Many of the most prominent families of Santa Fe invested heavily in the overland trade. Yearly they made up their own caravans, braved the hazards of the trail, and purchased American goods at Independence or even St. Louis for resale in New Mexico and Chihuahua. In this they had an edge, being exempt from the heavy import duties imposed upon their American competitors. One of those Catholic merchants, or a member of his wagon crew, had dropped the medal turned up by Claude Unruh's plow.

Beyond Cottonwood Crossing, westbound travelers struck the Arkansas River near the present town of Great Bend. Now they were approaching the arid uplands that tilted toward them from the base of the mountains still far beyond the horizon. By keeping close to the river on the next leg of their journey, they were assured of adequate water for themselves and their stock. But that comforting fact was overshadowed by the growing danger of Indian raiders.

Pawnee Rock, among the best-known landmarks on the trail, offered ideal cover for an ambush. From its summit, reported the soldier-writer Henry Inman, feathered warriors could "dash down upon the Santa Fe traders like hawks, to carry off their plunder and their scalps." Almost every yard of brown sod at the base of the rock, he contended, covered a skeleton. Standing on the smooth crest under a piercing Kansas sun, I felt a sudden chill at the thought that scores of unremembered tragedies had taken place here.

Just below Pawnee Rock the trail reached the Pawnee Fork, a tributary of the Arkansas. Not far away, the Army in 1859 built Fort Larned to guard the vulnerable merchant caravans and to provide escort service for mail riders. Of the several posts placed in western Kansas to protect the Santa Fe road, Fort Larned was the most important and is today the best preserved. As I wandered among the buildings and across the parade ground, all carefully tended by the National Park Service, it was easy to picture stalwart men swinging into the saddle and, amid the clank of arms, riding forth on patrol.

Indians, of course, were not the only danger on the trail. Something we scarcely consider now was much to be feared: the prairie

Grave of a drover who worked the trail from 1855 to 1863 lies near New Mexico's Wagon Mound, once a familiar landmark to passing teamsters. Suggesting the shape of a prairie schooner, the mountain loomed on the horizon signaling travelers that Santa Fe lay 100 miles beyond.

LOWELL GEORGIA

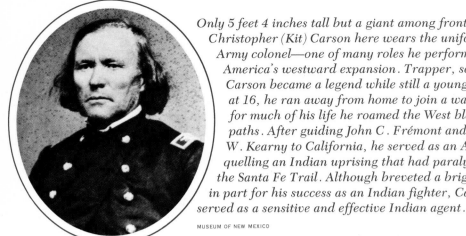

Only 5 feet 4 inches tall but a giant among frontiersmen, Christopher (Kit) Carson here wears the uniform of a Union Army colonel—one of many roles he performed during America's westward expansion. Trapper, scout, and soldier, Carson became a legend while still a young man. In 1826, at 16, he ran away from home to join a wagon train, and for much of his life he roamed the West blazing new paths. After guiding John C. Frémont and then Stephen W. Kearny to California, he served as an Army officer, quelling an Indian uprising that had paralyzed traffic on the Santa Fe Trail. Although breveted a brigadier general in part for his success as an Indian fighter, Carson also served as a sensitive and effective Indian agent.

MUSEUM OF NEW MEXICO

fire. Some blazes were started by lightning, others by red men who used to drive off pestering mosquitoes with smoke or trap deer with flames. Careless cooks from the wagon trains were also sometimes the culprits, letting their campfires escape.

"The [perils of] these prairie conflagrations . . . when the grass is tall and dry . . . [can be] sufficient to daunt the stoutest heart." That was Josiah Gregg's judgment after his own close brush with disaster. Jim Beckwourth, a famous black mountain man, horse thief, and part-time courier for the military, carried dispatches over the trail in 1848. Arriving at Santa Fe in December, he related that "there was little snow on the prairie and grass was burned from Pawnee Fork to Council Grove," a distance of 150 miles.

One August afternoon I had a firsthand view of the frightening power of a prairie fire. Topping a hill in my car, I caught sight of a dense cloud of smoke billowing along a three-mile strip of horizon. As I approached, the air grew hot and acrid. On the perimeter of the fire, a line of men beat down the encroaching tongues of flame with wet sacks. It was not hard to imagine the dread felt by early wagoners who, like Gregg, were pursued by one of these ravenous infernos.

Three miles east of Fort Larned stands the Santa Fe Trail Center, a museum and research facility of the Fort Larned Historical Society. Director Bill Pitts and archaeologist Earl Monger agreed to show me traces of the old trail still visible in the surrounding countryside. We bounced over farm roads, ferreting out ruts, fords, a buffalo wallow or two, and. even a prairie-dog colony, all of which would have been familiar to the Santa Fe pioneers. At a weed-filled flat on Ash Creek, we stopped the car. "This is the spot," Earl said, "where Susan Magoffin tipped over in her Rockaway. The injuries she suffered undermined her health and led to a miscarriage later at Bent's Fort. It's a sad place."

I recalled the passage in Susan's journal that tells of the mishap—how the vehicle "whirled completely over with a perfect crash . . . [and was] entirely broken to pieces." Her husband carried the stunned girl to the shade of a tree, and revived her by rubbing whiskey on hands and face. Now I was standing on the very ground where that small drama had unfolded more than a century past.

Maj. Gen. Stephen Watts Kearny holds a controversial place in the history of the Southwest. Dispatched in 1846 by President James K. Polk to conquer New Mexico and California during the Mexican War, Kearny crossed the plains and occupied Santa Fe without bloodshed. While some credit Kearny's leadership for this feat, others suggest that recognition should go to a Santa Fe trader who negotiated the takeover with the corrupt provincial governor. After establishing a civil administration, Kearny ordered the codification that still forms the basis of state law in New Mexico. The newly promoted brigadier general then pressed on to California, where he helped Commodore Robert F. Stockton pacify that territory.

From the vicinity of Fort Larned, the wagons often formed into four parallel columns. This was done, one trader explained, because when the train moved in one long file "the march is continually inter-rupted; for every accident which delays a wagon ahead stops all those behind. By marching four abreast . . . the wagons can also be thrown more readily into a condition of defense. . . ." Other diarists pointed out that moving in four lines meant more drivers were in front, out of the lung-stinging dust churned up by the heavy wheels. Having lived through many seasons of New Mexico dust storms, I could appreciate the teamsters' distaste for flying grit.

Higher up the Arkansas Valley, past the site where Dodge City would take root in the early '70's, the merchants came to a fork in the trail. There, at what became known as the Cimarron crossing of the Arkansas, a crucial decision had to be made. Should they take the shorter Cimarron cutoff with its scant water and acute danger from hostile Indians? Or was it wiser to follow the more northerly moun-tain branch, enduring the extra miles for a chance to rest and pur-chase supplies at Bent's Fort? Most of the caravans, it seems, were in a hurry, and chose the faster desert route.

That was the case with an 1828 wagon train of which Milton Bry-an was a member. "Crossing the Arkansas River," he reported, "[we entered] upon the great American Desert which was lying beyond as listless, lonesome, and noiseless as a sleeping sea."

In Bryan's day, every man looked to the filling of the water bar-rels in his wagon, for the wide and unfenced land ahead, as yet un-broken by a plow, was painfully dry. Today the same terrain of southwest Kansas shows a remarkable transformation. The "noise-lessness" has succumbed to the chug-chug of irrigation pumps, and the boundless, short-grass prairie has given way to fields of maize, wheat, and soybeans. The emptiness, too, has been broken up: by farm towns with tree-vaulted streets and green parks, and by tower-ing grain elevators topped by colored beacons that wink in the night.

For the plucky merchants, the ordeal by thirst came to an end at the Cimarron River. Late in the season, its intermittent flow of water was apt to be heavy with alkali, so chalky white that some men de-clared it an excellent substitute for milk. But it sustained travelers and their livestock, and caravans stuck to its sandy, near-treeless

Ox-drawn wagons churn up dust on the parched road to Santa Fe in a 1904 painting by Frederic Remington. On the early-19th-century door panel at right, an unknown artist portrayed a familiar southwestern sight—a New Mexican buffalo hunter and his horse. Such ciboleros *could "hunt like the wild Indians," observed Josiah Gregg admiringly in the book* Commerce of the Prairies.

banks for several days as they pressed on in a southwesterly course toward Santa Fe. Following in their path, I walked out on the bleached crust of the dry riverbed and gazed at a shrunken pool—all that existed, along this stretch, of the much-vaunted Cimarron. Its foul odor made me glad of the cold, fresh water I carried in my car.

To get to Bent's Fort on the Arkansas River, midway along the northern branch of the trail, I had to do a bit of backtracking. But unlike some of the hurried traders, I refused to bypass the pearl of the Santa Fe Trail. Bent's Fort was not a military post, but a private fur-trading establishment built in 1833-34 by the mercantile firm of Bent, St. Vrain & Company. Its location in southeastern Colorado, not far from the mouth of the Purgatoire, was at a wilderness crossroads. Long-haired trappers in greasy buckskins ranging up and down the Rockies knocked at its gate. Members of the principal Indian tribes of the western plains paused there to trade. Trails from the distant Yellowstone and Platte converged at Bent's.

The trading post was also the rendezvous in 1846 for dragoons of Stephen Watts Kearny's Army of the West, which had been charged at the outbreak of the Mexican War with the mission of seizing New Mexico. After a taxing march over the Santa Fe Trail from Fort Leavenworth, Kearny's nearly exhausted men took a welcome rest at the fort. It offered such unaccustomed luxuries as a whiskey called Taos Lightning, and a billiard table covered with green baize.

A first view of the massive adobe fort, tucked in a sheltered bend of the Arkansas, is as impressive today as it must have been to the Santa Fe traders, mountain men, and soldiers. It is not the same structure now, but an excellent reconstruction on the old foundations carried out by the National Park Service in 1975 and 1976 and officially dubbed Bent's Old Fort. "We had a number of original plans and drawings of the place," Superintendent John Patterson told me as we sat under a long porch roof facing the cool interior courtyard. "For that reason, it's safe to say that our reconstruction is 95 percent authentic. Lt. James W. Abert, a topographical engineer attached to Kearny's army, made complete measurements. We even know the correct dimensions of the flagpole."

From Bent's Fort, the Santa Fe Trail carried travelers down to high and stony Raton Pass, whose northern entrance was conspicuously marked by flat-topped Fishers Peak. In the thinning air at the summit, the Yankee traders halted briefly to gaze upon the velvet plains ahead. Once over the pass, as they well knew, it was a matter of easy stages southward to a link-up with the Cimarron cutoff.

A few days more and the New Mexico settlements rose close at hand. In the first of any consequence, Las Vegas, the townsfolk gathered on a scorching day in August 1846. They had come to hear General Kearny, surrounded by his well-armed troops, declare that their province was henceforth part of the United States. The message, spoken through an interpreter, was received with silent resignation.

Pressing forward, Kearny followed the tracks of the freight wagons through the villages of Tecolote and San *(Continued on page 38)*

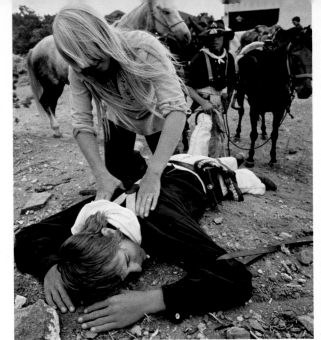

The trail revisited:
fifty-seven days in the saddle

Following the median strip of a superhighway, riders trace the Santa Fe Trail near Glorieta Pass in New Mexico. The group covered all 900 miles of the historic route on horseback during a 57-day journey in 1978. As with 19th-century caravans, the trip proved a stern test of endurance. Blistering heat, violent windstorms, and shortage of water challenged riders and mounts along the way. Typically rising at 5 a.m. and traveling till the heat became intolerable, the group averaged 20 miles a day. After long hours in the saddle, a weary cavalryman (left) gets a back rub. For Casey Meyers (far left), the exploit required special determination: He broke his leg before the trip began, and rode almost the entire distance wearing a cast.

Journey's end: Bearing American flags of 1848 and 1978, the travelers gather before the Spanish governor's residence in the Plaza de Santa Fe, the traditional marketplace. Hundreds of spectators gathered here more than a century ago to meet incoming wagon trains. "The arrival," wrote Gregg in his book, "produced a great deal of bustle and excitement among the natives. . . . crowds of women and boys flocked around." Extending a welcome to group leader Allan Maybee, Mayor Art Trujillo adds his name to a roll signed by the mayor of every town along the route. At right, rider Rhonda Ellwood, from Kansas, greets her two-year-old sister, Krysti.

At El Rancho de las Golondrinas, a living-history museum south of Santa Fe, Domingo Perea steadies pack burros during a two-day harvest fiesta. In addition to firewood and chili peppers,

LOWELL GEORGIA

typical items found in the plaza market in colonial times, the animals' load includes canvas-covered casks of water—a necessity for any extended travel in the arid region.

37

Miguel. Beyond the ruined pueblo and mission of Pecos, his column threaded Glorieta Pass, and on August 18 he entered Santa Fe without firing a shot. Down came the Mexican tricolor. In its place, on the rooftop of the old Spanish Palace of the Governors, the American flag unfurled in the breeze.

The invasion and annexation of New Mexico brought fundamental change to the Santa Fe Trail. No longer was it a road connecting two nations. Now it became one of the principal highways binding America's East to the infant West. The volume of trade steadily increased. By the early '50's, new mail and stagecoach service contributed to the growing traffic.

When the Indians continued to hammer at the trail, the government responded with new military posts. The most ambitious of these near the western end of the trail was Fort Union, begun in 1851. By the latter '60's, its adobe barracks, shops, and warehouses sprawled across 74 acres, and it kept troopers constantly in the field.

But the days of the Santa Fe Trail were numbered. As the railroads extended across the continent, freighting by oxen and mule team grew obsolete. The Atchison, Topeka and Santa Fe Railroad reached Dodge City in 1872, and Trinidad, Colorado, at the foot of Raton Pass, in 1878. Each advance to a new railhead meant a further shrinking of the old trail. On February 14, 1880, a Santa Fe newspaper, celebrating the arrival of the rails, spread an epitaph in bold type across its front page: *The Old Santa Fe Trail Passes Into Oblivion*.

Standing one morning in the tree-shaded plaza, close by a monument marking the end of the trail, I decided that the obituary of 1880 with its reference to "oblivion" had been premature. Along with a crowd of history-minded Santa Fe citizens, I was awaiting the arrival of a party of nine men and women who were completing a 57-day horseback ride from Independence over the old route.

Soon they rounded a corner and entered the square, their horses' steel-shod hooves ringing on the hard pavement. The mayor delivered a welcome in front of the adobe residence of the Spanish governors—the very spot where General Kearny received the surrender of the city in 1846. In appropriate garb, the tired, dusty riders with 900 miles behind them looked as if they had just passed through a time warp. The spectators at my elbows were impressed. For a few moments they felt, as I did, the splendid reality of what it must mean to ride, as in times long past, the entire length of the Santa Fe Trail.

Allan Maybee, the party's leader, uttered a few quiet words. His broad shoulders straining a fringed buckskin jacket, he spoke about rekindling the spirit of the trail and commemorating the deeds of those businessmen in wagons who had made the long march across the bleak plains. And he commented, almost as an afterthought, on how quickly prairie and mountain can lay hold on one's affections.

The real tribute to the Santa Fe Trail and its builders was not in Allan Maybee's speech, but in the achievement he and his companions had recorded. The old westering urge that drove the Santa Fe traders, the Oregon homeseekers, and the California forty-niners has not entirely left us. That magnetic pull lingers still.

BOTH BY LOWELL GEORGIA

Diminutive spectator awaits the start of a religious procession during the harvest festival at El Rancho de las Golondrinas. Steeped in Spanish and Indian traditions, the fiesta includes performances by folk dancers such as Angela Manzanares (opposite), member of a college group from Colorado.

Road to Destiny

By Wallace Stegner

*Guidebooks lured
emigrants with
dramatic descriptions
of the journey to
Oregon, and offered
advice on preparations.
J. M. Shively crossed
the continent twice
before producing his
1846 volume (below).*

We grind up a steep gravel road through the sagebrush toward the crest of a ridge, and park at the top before a pavilion fitted out with historical exhibits. Behind us the gray, sage-covered Snake River plain spreads endlessly east, south, and west. The canyon of the Snake is out there somewhere, sunk below the flat surrounding surface, invisible. Human developments are few and meager; even the diagonal streak of Interstate Highway 80N is a mere detail in all that emptiness. We are above the noise. I can sense only the wind and time.

To the north, the Boise Mountains are a ragged outline on the horizon. Directly opposite us across the valley, the Boise River emerges from the barren mountains and meanders in a green line toward the city of Boise, 10 or 12 miles to the northwest. Straight down the gray hill on which we stand, the ruts of the Oregon Trail, plainly visible after nearly a century of disuse, head in a beeline for the river. Here, for a few minutes, every wagon train that helped make that track must have paused to look ahead and get its wind.

Legend says that in the 1830's U. S. Army Captain Benjamin Louis Eulalie de Bonneville stood on this ridge and cried out happily, *"Le bois! Le bois! Voyez le bois!"*—thus giving a name to the river and eventually to Idaho's capital city. Whether he said that or not, the ridge has long been called Bonneville Point. If he didn't shout his pleasure at the sight of the timbered stream, others did. Diary after pioneer diary blesses the few pleasant days on the Boise.

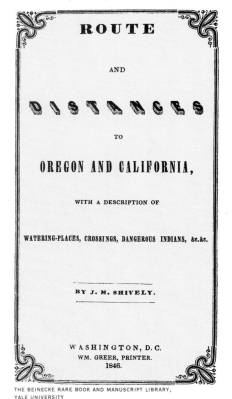

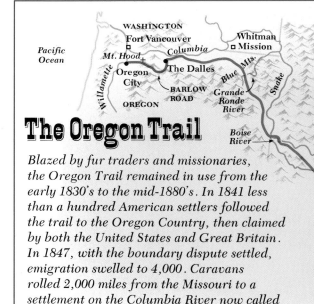

The Oregon Trail

*Blazed by fur traders and missionaries,
the Oregon Trail remained in use from the
early 1830's to the mid-1880's. In 1841 less
than a hundred American settlers followed
the trail to the Oregon Country, then claimed
by both the United States and Great Britain.
In 1847, with the boundary dispute settled,
emigration swelled to 4,000. Caravans
rolled 2,000 miles from the Missouri to a
settlement on the Columbia River now called
The Dalles. To reach the Willamette Valley,
emigrants rafted down the Columbia gorge
until the Barlow Road opened in 1846.*

John C. Frémont's exploring expedition looked down from this hill on October 7, 1843, and that evening Frémont recorded: "... the *Rivière Boisée* ... is a beautiful rapid stream, with clear mountain water, and, as the name indicates, well wooded with some varieties of timber—among which are handsome cottonwoods. Such a stream had become quite a novelty ... and we were delighted this afternoon to make a pleasant camp under fine old trees again."

Frémont's *Report*, widely used as a guidebook by later companies, gave parched travelers something to look forward to. The road got harder as endurance and spirits failed. It helped to have a few days of easy going before the trials of the Burnt River Canyon and the Blue Mountains.

The hardships, the fortitude, the achievements of the emigrants who traveled this long road are in our minds as we stand in the October sun on Bonneville Point. The history of the trail is the subject of the display panels that my hosts—Wally Meyer of the Bureau of Land Management and Judy Austin and Larry Jones of the Idaho State Historical Society—have had a hand in setting up.

"We've only been involved a few years—since the Bicentennial," Wally Meyer tells me. "The Bureau of Land Management had never been able to get into the recreation business, or interpretation, or historic preservation, mainly because of budget. But under the Federal Land Policy and Management Act of 1976, we're beginning to develop a program. A big part of the Oregon Trail remnants are on

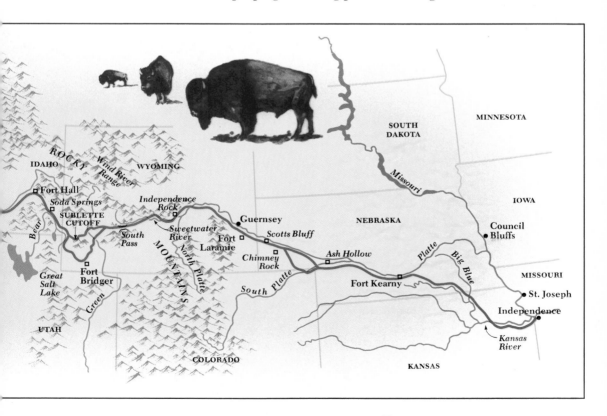

*Pioneers inch their
way up a steep passage
in a lithograph based
on a mural in the U.S.
Capitol. In 1845
journalist John L.
O'Sullivan sanctified
American determination
to "overspread the
continent allotted by
Providence" when he
coined the term "our
manifest destiny."*

our land, so we're the natural agency to coordinate its preservation."

And the bureau's activities have stimulated renewed interest in other quarters. On this trip I have seen similar exhibits and other monuments, sponsored by both public and private organizations, at strategic places all the way from Independence to Oregon City. The great road of western settlement, ignored and half forgotten for several generations, is becoming a road of pilgrimage.

For me this national heritage is also a personal one. In nearly 60 years I have traversed it dozens of times, by rail, auto, thumb, from the time when much of it was unpaved dirt road to the time of the six-lane superhighway. Childhood trips from town to a dry-land homestead taught me how it feels to jolt and lurch for hours across burnouts and prairie dog holes, down through coulees, across quicksandy streams, in a springless wagon. I know why emigrants walked whenever they could.

The western two-thirds of the trail runs through my native coun-

try. Its colors and distances are what I recognize; its hard, brilliant light is the first light I remember. I know its heat and dust and weathers. I have shared the common emigrant experience of being caught out in one of the Platte Valley's terrifying electrical storms, stumbling around in the streaming dark with the tent down and the lightning so close and incessant that it stunned the senses. And if I never sat out one of those storms in a covered wagon, I *have* done so in a 1919 Model T Ford, the isinglass side curtains blown out, the magneto box crackling with blue sparks, my hair on end with static and the singed air smelling of ozone. "Well," my father said afterward, "that wasn't exactly like going to hell, but it was close."

I know how it is to be on the road for weeks at a time, without motels or roadside conveniences. I have felt the tedium, the discomfort; but I also know the exhilaration of fine mornings with fair-weather clouds, and have soaked in the good sounds: music around a campfire, the soft call of a mourning dove during a drowsy hot nooning, the rattle of cottonwood leaves. And I have dragged my share of gunnysacks around, gathering cow chips if not buffalo chips, for fires in the woodless country.

So I think I understand this national experience of the trail in personal ways. Up here on Bonneville Point, it comes over me anew. There go the white-topped wagons down the gray hill. There go the skillful drivers, the patient passengers, the restless outriders. This place, like many others I have seen marked and protected along the 2,000 miles of the trail, is dense with their history and their hope. The wheel marks heading purposefully for the river are the tracks of a strenuous dream.

Go back to a time of exaggerated national growing pains. In 1803 the United States consisted of 17 states plus other territory that at no point extended west of the Mississippi. The Louisiana Purchase, ratified on October 20, 1803, immediately doubled the nation's area and jumped its western boundary to the crest of the Rocky Mountains.

Beyond the crest, south of some undefined line, was New Spain. On the north, everything from the Rockies to the sea was "the Oregon Country." America's claim to it dated from a May day in 1792 when Capt. Robert Gray ventured into the mouth of an unknown river which he named after his ship, the *Columbia*. The British, close behind, actually explored the river more thoroughly than he did, and thus had their own claim to support the North West Company and Hudson's Bay Company in their efforts to control the region's fur trade. Temporarily, the two nations agreed to joint occupation.

The British wanted everything down to the north bank of the Columbia; American expansionists thought the United States should run north well into what is now British Columbia. While the dispute went on, so did vigorous exploration and exploitation. Alexander Mackenzie's trip in 1793 over the Canadian Rockies and down wild rivers to the Pacific was a major effort on the British side, as the Lewis and Clark expedition of 1804-06 was on the American.

"Too thick to drink, too thin to plow"

Braided channels of the Platte River reflect the low morning sun near Fort Kearny, Nebraska. Too shallow for riverboats, the complex Platte offered a lifeline of water and forage for wagon trains heading west. Described by one observer in 1834 as "two to three miles wide and fully knee deep," the river nonetheless held peril for those crossing it. Currents and quicksand defeated many a drover and his livestock. Refuting a traveler who derided the river as an "infernal liar . . . hardly able to float a canoe," today's paddlers (below) move tranquilly through strands of the northern fork of the river near North Platte, Nebraska.

But neither journey, however heroic and important, established a transcontinental road. The Oregon Trail was actually blazed eastward, when Robert Stuart led a party of American fur traders from Astoria, on the Columbia River, back to the Missouri by way of South Pass in 1812-13. Jedediah Smith and other mountain men rediscovered the pass from the east in 1824, and continued westward in Stuart's track. From then until the railroad took a more direct route in 1868, South Pass was the gateway to the West.

Once established, the trail would doom all efforts of the British to hold Oregon—in spite of the fact that the Yankees lost the struggle for the northwestern fur trade. The American post at Astoria, built in 1811, was taken over by the Montreal-based North West Company during the War of 1812. Even before the Nor'Westers and the Hudson's Bay Company fused in 1821, brigades of British traders had begun their penetration into the remote tributaries of the Columbia.

The Americans, instead of establishing a network of wilderness trading posts to buy Indian furs, as the British did, dispersed white trappers in the mountains. Then they brought everyone together at an annual rendezvous, usually in the vicinity of the Green River. Here the mountain men were supplied with the powder, lead, traps, tobacco, guns, knives, and hatchets needed for another season, and their Indian wives with mirrors, needles, beads, and scarlet cloth. When the company trappers had drunk up their wages and the free trappers their credit, they went back into the mountains with their hangovers and their Indian friends, while the company caravans crawled toward the Missouri loaded with beaver pelts.

But whenever the Americans tried to compete with the British on the Columbia, they lost. From 1837 on, the major posts beyond the Continental Divide on which Oregon emigrants could depend for supplies, fresh animals, and services were British: Fort Hall, originally American; old Fort Boise at the mouth of the Boise River; Fort Walla Walla; and, of course, Fort Vancouver, from which base the hospitable and magnanimous John McLoughlin, Hudson's Bay Company representative, aided many an American party that arrived broken down and starving at The Dalles.

The fur trade lasted only a generation before the streams were trapped out, the beaver-hat business replaced by the silk-hat business, the mountains overtaken by other kinds of travelers. The last rendezvous, a sadly diminished one, took place in 1840. By then, fur traders and missionaries between them had completed the road down which those fulfilling America's manifest destiny would pour.

There is no visible vestige of old Fort Boise now. But at the farming village of Parma, Idaho, I drive off the highway to sit for a few minutes at the quiet meeting of rivers where the fastidious missionary bride Narcissa Whitman, by then confirmed in pregnancy, could wash her clothes for only the third time since leaving the Missouri frontier three months and 1,500 miles before. That single fact suggests how long and difficult a camping trip the Oregon Trail was—how dirty clothes would get; how frequently boils would erupt

"Every-where-present angel of mercy," a friend called missionary-physician Marcus Whitman. Until their deaths in 1847 at the hands of Cayuse Indians who blamed them for a measles epidemic, the couple made their mission quarters a haven for thousands of travel-weary emigrants. They adopted 11 children—including one family of seven—orphaned on the trail. Drury Haight based his paintings of the Whitmans on pencil sketches by the Canadian artist Paul Kane, who visited the mission in July 1847.

on unwashed necks; how often travelers heavily armed against buffalo, wolves, and usually peaceful Indians would accidentally shoot themselves or one another; how many people and animals would drown at river crossings. And how many times animals or wagons would break down; how many people would suffer dysentery and cholera; how many children doped with heat and fatigue on long afternoons would fall off wagons and be run over by iron-shod wheels; how often rattlesnakes would bite animals, which generally died, and people, who generally did not, but lay sick for days or weeks.

Today, driving good roads in an air-conditioned car, it is easy to forget the bond with the earth and the earth's hardships that wagon travelers had, and how commonplace those hardships—and dangers—were. The rattlesnakes, for one example. I have seen none on the whole trip. But I remember a time in 1921 when, marooned by a cloudburst, my family spent a night with a homesteader just east of the Continental Divide. When we left, he called my brother and me aside and invited us to choose from a *pailful* of snake rattles he had collected in a single summer. "Take a lot," he said. "Take a handful. There's plenty more where those came from."

All wagon trains, even the ones traveling the trail almost up to the turn of the century, endured those hazards—and after the mid-1850's, when the emigration began to alienate tribes previously peaceful, occasional Indian trouble as well. For the missionaries and their wives, the passage was further complicated by jealousy, personal dislikes, and most unchristian feelings.

When a delegation of Nez Percés appeared in St. Louis in 1831 asking that someone be sent to teach them the great medicine of the white man's Book, they probably did not distinguish between Anglicans, reports of whose mission school had impressed them, and Catholic "black robes" they had heard about from fur traders and Iroquois trappers. But it was Protestants who responded first.

Methodist Jason Lee, with several companions, started west in 1834 and eventually reached the Willamette Valley, which he liked so well that he set up his mission there, not among the Nez Percés but among the Chinooks.

The next year Samuel Parker, a Congregationalist, accompanied by the Presbyterian physician Marcus Whitman, went out to the trappers' rendezvous with the American Fur Company caravan. There they had a memorable introduction to wilderness life. Of the white men living in the mountains, perhaps 200 were present, along with hundreds of Indians and a Scottish sportsman, Sir William Stewart, on his annual safari. Whitman and Parker witnessed some Beowulfian carousing, saw Kit Carson kill a bullying braggart named Shunar in a duel, preached to those sober enough to listen, and found the Nez Percés and Flatheads eager for instruction. Whitman, who took on a lively surgical practice, removed from Jim Bridger's back a three-inch iron arrowhead he had carried in his flesh for three years. "In the mountains," Jim told the doctor, "meat don't spoil."

Sure now that a Nez Percé mission was wanted, Whitman returned east, taking with him two Indian boys to be educated and to

*Summer squall bursts out of the north over Ash Hollow, Nebraska, where wagon trains eased
down a precipitous hill to find water, forage, and the last wood for wagon repairs for more than a*

hundred miles. "Black, black it rises. . . . the forked lightning . . . seems to drop to the ground,"
wrote a woman on the trail in 1853 as she faced a similar storm sweeping across the Great Plains.

assist him in raising funds and support. Parker went on to the Pacific and finally returned home by ship. The book he wrote about the West, *Journal of an Exploring Tour beyond the Rocky Mountains,* was to have a powerful effect on the settlement of Oregon.

Marcus Whitman wrote no book, and his wife, Narcissa, left only her journal and letters. But the two had an even greater influence on the future, and their adventure became one of the great tragic stories of our history.

Narcissa Prentiss, 26, was auburn-haired and beautiful, deeply religious, and passionate to be a missionary. The American Board of Foreign Missions had already rejected her plea to go to the Nez Percés (What? Send an unmarried woman among savages?) when Marcus Whitman, who had heard about her interest from Parker, paid her a call. He promptly fell in love, and proposed. She agreed to marry him only if he would take her west.

The mission board's approval hinged on finding a second couple to go along. By an irony no fiction writer would dare invent, the only pair available were Henry Harmon Spalding and his wife, Eliza.

Spalding was a moody and difficult divine who had himself attempted to win Narcissa and been refused. Scalded with humiliation, he had turned to the shy, ill-favored, kind Eliza Hart. Through four exhausting months on the trail, the Whitmans shared their honeymoon tent not only with Narcissa's rejected suitor and his frail wife, but also with the pretentious and insufferable handyman-missionary William Gray, who in later years wrote and distorted the history of Oregon.

Narcissa and Eliza were the first white women to cross the continent, the first many of the mountain men had seen in years, the first the Indians had ever seen. Once the missionary party caught up with a fur traders' caravan that had refused to wait for them, Narcissa tried to make a lark of the tedious and uncomfortable but relatively easy trip up the Platte Valley. Where poor Eliza was reduced nearly to invalidism, Narcissa was eager, interested, and game. Indians crowded to stare and finger their clothes. At the mountain men's rendezvous, the Indian wives stood in line to plant wet kisses on them. They were a sensation, and an omen: the first drop in the family migration that would soon be a trickle and in a few years a flood.

With hoarse shouting and cracking whips, teamsters in the 1867 painting "California Crossing" ford the South Platte River near Julesburg, Colorado. The year before, artist William Henry Jackson saw the river "filled from bank to bank" with teams. "Sometimes even eighteen yoke [of oxen] were used" to drag a single wagon over the "shifty quicksand."

"Like the blades of grass in spring," one Sioux leader called the growing numbers of white men intruding on his tribal lands. In Charles M. Russell's painting "Watching the Settlers" (above), a hunting party of Plains Indians surveys a wagon train. In "A Doubtful Visitor," Russell shows a brave confronting an emigrant family—perhaps to demand a toll.

Marcus Whitman's wagon was also an omen. The fur caravans had used wagons and carts ever since 1830, but most wheels stopped at Fort Laramie. Whitman wanted to take a set the whole way.

He nearly killed himself trying. In a notable understatement, Narcissa wrote somewhere near the Bear River that "husband" was "not as fleshy" as he had been. No wonder. In 1836 there was no semblance of a wagon road beyond Fort Laramie. Every creek crossing was an ordeal of unloading, disassembling, fording, reloading. In the dry air, wooden wheels shrank and iron tires fell off. No one had ever dug down the banks, or cleared the stumps, or thrown rocks out of the track. When the wagon stuck in Smith Fork, Narcissa hoped that husband would give it up—but he got it out and hauled it on. When he broke an axle, she rejoiced. Now he would surely have to abandon the vehicle. Instead, he made it into a two-wheeled cart which he took clear to Fort Boise! Only there did the Hudson's Bay Company people finally persuade him to leave it behind.

By that time, even Narcissa's spirits had been eroded by exhaustion, dust, heat, sagebrush (which she hated with a passion), pregnancy, and the difficult association with the Spaldings. Eliza was a meek bundle of suffering; Henry was grim. Relations between the men of God had broken down into bitter antipathy. In the Blue Mountains they seized on an excuse to part company, and arrived separately at Fort Walla Walla. And when, after a spell of John McLoughlin's hospitality at Fort Vancouver, they set out to build their mission, they built two, so they would not have to work together. The Spaldings went to the Nez Percés at Lapwai, on the Clearwater near present-day Lewiston, Idaho. The Whitmans went to Waiilatpu, on the Walla Walla, among the Cayuses.

Now the door to Oregon was open. Twice in 1837 Jason Lee's Willamette mission was reinforced by sea; and the next spring Lee went back to the States and stumped for settlers, plows, farm animals, sawmill machinery, everything needed to people the country and frustrate the British. He carried a petition signed by 36 of the 51 residents of the Willamette Valley—the second of several such petitions—asking the United States to "take formal and speedy possession" of the disputed territory. He also carried a joint letter from Whitman and Spalding asking for help. Their request fitted into the national mood like an arm into a sleeve. Emigration societies were already beginning to form.

In the summer of 1838 there were more missionaries: William Gray, now newly married; Asa Smith, also married and as insufferable as Gray; the Cushing Eells and Elkanah Walker families, who might have made it through in reasonable amity if it had not been for the bad feeling between Gray and Smith. As it was, Mary Walker wrote in her journal, "We have a strange company of Missionaries. Scarcely one who is not intolerable on some account." Later on, pregnant, underfed, overworked, suffering from dysentery, she sat in the rain and cried to think how comfortable her father's hogs were, back in Maine.

Lessons in history start early in Gering, Nebraska. For their pioneer garb, 5-year-old Wade Simpson and his sister, Shannon, 6, won a first prize in their town's annual Oregon Trail Days. Gering has honored the early settlers for the last 58 years.

When they finally reached Waiilatpu, they crowded Narcissa Whitman's little house with their hatreds, and had to be distributed carefully to keep them from each other's throats.

In 1842, when the mission board ordered the closing of all but one of its bickering Oregon missions, Marcus Whitman made a heroic winter trip east and persuaded the board to reverse its decision. Preparing to return to Oregon in May 1843, he found gathered on the banks of the Kansas River nearly a thousand people, including more than a hundred families, a great assortment of wagons, and 5,000 cattle, ready for the trail. He also found Lieutenant Frémont, who had traveled as far as South Pass the year before, assembling a party to reconnoiter all the way to the Columbia.

Whitman acted as a guide and adviser to the "Great Migration" of 1843, urging its participants on, encouraging them, driving them. His voice hammered constantly: "Travel, travel, travel! Nothing else will take you to the end of your journey; nothing is wise that does not help you along. Nothing is good for you that causes a moment's delay." He had to leave them before the end, and they got into trouble on the Columbia and were rescued by dependable John McLoughlin. But they played out their role in the drama of manifest destiny.

Four more companies totaling about 1,500 emigrants came in 1844, and nearly twice that number in 1845. In 1846 the Mexican War inhibited travel; but in that "year of decision," as critic-historian Bernard De Voto called it, the United States and Great Britain compromised the Oregon question and set the international boundary at the 49th parallel.

Oregon was won, and Marcus Whitman had more to do with winning it than any other, for he had demonstrated the feasibility of taking wheels across the continent. Yet the fate that had already brought tragedy to him and Narcissa—their daughter, the first all-white child born in Oregon, had drowned at the age of two—soon struck again. In payment for their devoted service to the heathen, the Whitmans were blamed for white men's diseases that broke out among the Cayuses. On November 29, 1847, they and 11 others were killed. The brave and patient Narcissa was found shot and tomahawked, her long, auburn hair matted with blood, quirt lashes across her face. After she was buried, wolves dug her up and gnawed

Lifelong students of the Oregon Trail, Paul Henderson and his wife, Helen, stand almost in the shadow of Chimney Rock, Nebraska. For nearly 60 years—until his death in 1979 at the age of 83—the couple tirelessly explored the famous route.

her corpse. The black she had worn on a whim for her wedding was, as it turned out, sadly portentous.

After the discovery of gold in California in 1848, the "Oregon fever" subsided. Most of those who flooded the trail were headed for other destinations. Although Mormons migrating to Utah were a considerable part of the flood, the California-bound argonauts were overwhelmingly the most numerous. Army Maj. Osborne Cross, recording the march of mounted riflemen to garrison western posts in 1849, observed that only the sternest measures kept half the command from deserting wherever a California road turned off.

Meanwhile John McLoughlin, a good loser, had retired to live among and take the citizenship of the Americans who displaced him. His house on the bluff above the Willamette at Oregon City is now a national historic site. As I muse through it on this trip, it seems to me a very modest house for so big a man.

The route of the Oregon Trail was like a rope twisted hard in the middle and raveled at both ends. Its several beginning strands are now all but obliterated by farms, highways, or urban growth in and around Independence, Westport (now part of Kansas City), Fort Leavenworth, St. Joseph, Council Bluffs. The Independence and Westport strands follow or parallel the Santa Fe Trail to present-day Gardner, Kansas, where once—in the middle of a sea of grass—a track turned off to the right and a lonely sign read "Road to Oregon." Just west of the Big Blue River, near today's Marysville, the strands from Fort Leavenworth and St. Joseph twist in with the other two; and all go cross-country together, to dip down into the Platte Valley at the head of Grand Island. Along the north bank of the Platte comes the separate strand, beginning at Council Bluffs, that is usually called the Mormon Trail, but was used as well by fur traders and by trains bound for both Oregon and California.

The Platte Valley, though not treeless as it used to be, is still a direct, nearly level highway into the West. On this trip I follow the north bank generally, because that is where both Interstate 80 and U. S. 30 run; but the experience of the Platte Valley is and was the same on either side of the river.

Somewhere beyond reconstructed Fort Kearny, Nebraska, now

a historical park in the midst of cornfields, I pass the invisible line of the 100th meridian into the land of little rain. Here the diarists of the migrations began to report the cracking of lips and the drying-up of nostrils, the transition from turf to bunch grasses, the change of the earth's colors from greens to browns and tans, the sightings of unfamiliar animals—bison, pronghorns, jackrabbits, prairie dogs, horned toads—and the dry clarity of light that made distances deceptive. For the emigrants, each new day brought strangeness and wonder. The excitement of the unknown touched them all, for they were all—the mountain men excluded—greenhorns and amateurs.

I feel each change, too, but as recognition, not strangeness. A hitchhiker I pick up near North Platte makes me all the more aware of those feelings. He is a big blond fellow, once a football player for the University of Oregon, whose football days were ended by an automobile accident. Now he wears a steel hook where his right hand used to be. He is depressed, for his journey east in search of work or training has produced nothing, and he is going back in defeat along the route his great-grandparents traveled in hope. But before very long he begins to sniff the air and watch the country with a new eagerness. His senses obviously pick up something exciting. "Hey, it's beginning to smell like home!" he says. Home is Pendleton, Oregon, 1,200 miles away; but the boy is right. This does smell like home. When I drop him off, in order to visit Ash Hollow, his shoulders have a different set and his face a more alert look. Instead of standing by the highway with his thumb raised, he starts walking, as if he can't wait to shorten the distance remaining.

Ash Hollow is one of the great landmarks of the Oregon Trail. Coming down into it is Windlass Hill, a descent so hair-raising that— wrote one diarist—nobody in his company spoke a word for two

Respite from the rugged journey: Utah-bound emigrants commemorate with a group portrait their arrival at South Pass during the summer of 1866. The Oregon, Mormon, and California trails shared the broad saddle-like valley in Wyoming—one of the few places where wagons could breach the Rockies.

miles. Another reported, "I cannot say at what angle we descend but . . . some go as far as to say, 'the road hangs a little past the perpendicular!' " The old ruts, eroded by rains, have become a steep scar down the hillside. I try to imagine wagons coming down that slope, and cannot: even with wheels locked with chains, and every able-bodied person pulling back on ropes.

Beyond Ash Hollow, along the North Platte, some of the trail's most distinctive formations loom ahead—Courthouse Rock, the spire of Chimney Rock, Scotts Bluff. They moved emigrants to awe and bad poetry, and sharpened the sense of adventure.

The missionary Samuel Parker, passing through the area in 1835 before the name Courthouse Rock gained currency, wrote: "We encamped to-day in the neighborhood of a great natural curiosity, which, for the sake of a name, I shall call the old castle. It is situated up on the south side of the Platte, on a plain. . . . It has, at [a] distance . . . all the appearance of an old enormous building, somewhat dilapidated; but still you see the standing walls, the roof, the turrets, embrasures, the dome, and almost the very windows. . . ."

Scotts Bluff, whose distant prospect was described by the British adventurer Richard Burton as that of "a massive medieval city . . . round a colossal fortress," is now a national monument and a mine of Oregon Trail lore. Fort Laramie, a restoration of the frontier post, is even more worthy of a visit, for it was a bastion of the fur trade beginning in 1834, and after 1849 was the most strategic of the trail's military posts.

At Fort Laramie the two strands of the trail that have ascended the Platte are twisted tight. From here to the vicinity of the Little Sandy, west of South Pass, every wagon— *(Continued on page 64)*

Flashback: Modern-day "emigrants" stop for the night near Chimney Rock. Gordon Howard (center, in black hat) runs three-day wagon-train treks along a 45-mile section of the Oregon Trail in Nebraska. Participants wear the clothing of a century ago, and use authentic pioneer recipes for food cooked over open fires.

DAVID HISER

Living history at Fort Laramie

Fort Laramie still stands watch in the early-morning light of October. The sprawling post on the Wyoming plains marked the first third of the distance to Oregon. Between 1841 and 1866, an estimated 350,000 travelers passed this way. Many paused to mail letters home, repair wagons and equipment, and replenish provisions for the long push ahead. Inside today's restored fort, Lewis Eaton sometimes plays sutler as part of the National Park Service living-history program. At upper left, he points out some of the goods available at the post store, such as tobacco, whiskey, and rice—all at high prices. At left, Kelly Copper, in an 1870's riding costume, prepares for a gallop—one of the "few pleasures of an officer's wife," according to Eaton. Pat Frey adjusts the stirrup of her sidesaddle. At right: a cartridge box carried by a mid-19th-century soldier.

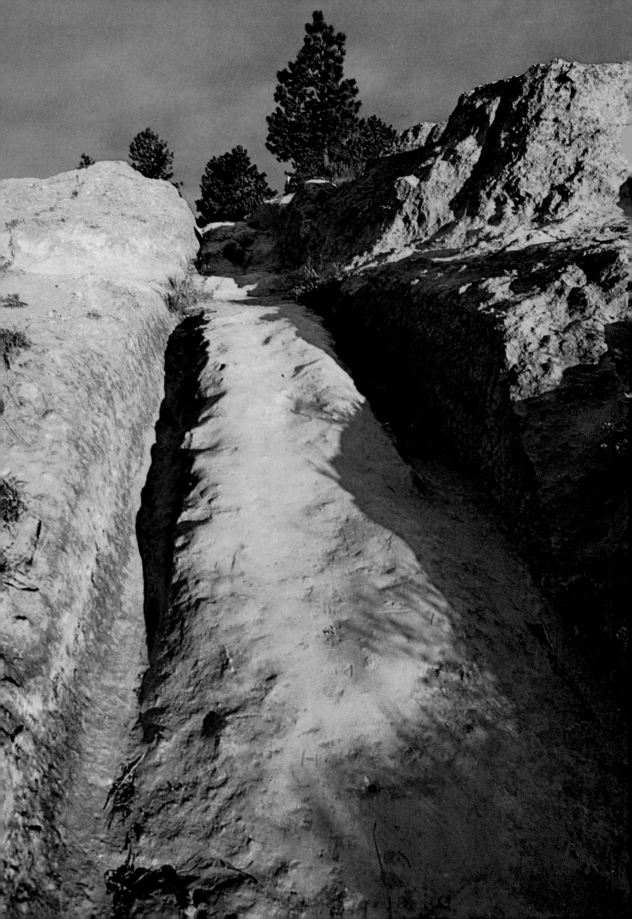

Landmarks of the trail

Ruts worn deep into sandstone silently attest to the thousands who struggled up this hill on the Oregon Trail near Guernsey, Wyoming. With all the hardships of the trip, emigrants nevertheless took time to visit landmarks such as Independence Rock, beside the Sweetwater River (below). Named by fur traders who celebrated the Fourth of July there in 1830, the granite monolith became the "great register of the desert." Travelers climbed the rock to scrawl or carefully incise their names (above) or to seek signs from home with "as much eagerness," one man noted, as if they found "letters in detail from long absent friends."

whether bound for Oregon, California, or the Salt Lake Valley—followed the same route, and for much of the way the same ruts. Opposite present-day Guernsey, Wyoming, where the trail lifted out of the river bottom, iron tires and animal hooves eventually wore down a channel five feet deep in the sandstone.

The emigrants used to race to make Independence Rock by the Fourth of July. For a day or two that pleasant camp on the Sweetwater was loud with gunfire, boisterous drinking, and patriotic oratory. But stopping there on another Independence Day, I see no more than a dozen cars and camper-vans in two hours. For today's picnickers the trail is actually much less crowded than it was for travelers of the 1840's and '50's.

Every wagon train tried to time its start so that spring grass would be sufficient to support its animals—without delaying so long that it risked early snows in the mountains. In consequence, everyone was on the road at once. The traveler's sight was always filled by long lines of wagons, pursuing their own course across the prairie. "During the first day's march there were at least twelve roads for twelve teams abreast," wrote emigrant Theodore Potter. Every desirable campground was a crowded, transitory, unsanitary town, complete with graveyard. Of the estimated 22,500 people who went to California in 1849, and the 45,000 who went in 1850, more than half each year passed Fort Kearny within a space of 15 days. Before and behind those cresting waves of men and animals, the road was nearly empty. In many places, it still is.

Beacon for the overlanders, the cleft of Split Rock cuts a ridge of Wyoming's Granite Mountains. Distinguishable for more than 50 miles on a clear day, Split Rock guided travelers to the Sweetwater River.

If Independence Rock is quiet, South Pass is almost moonlike in its emptiness. Once described as "a gateway more thronging than Gibraltar," the pass is again a wide, sagebrush plain sloping imperceptibly up toward the divide. An infrequent car moves across it. Instead of traffic, I see the white scuts of pronghorn antelope coasting along, and the shadows of hawks and clouds. And the two little hills, "notched crooked like a hind sight out of true," that still point a traveler westward into empty sky.

Beyond South Pass the rope began to fray again. From the Little Sandy, one road went southwest toward Fort Bridger, where it split into Utah and California-Oregon routes. Those travelers who elected not to swing down to Fort Bridger made a long, dry march by way of the Sublette cutoff to the Green, thence over the divide into the valley of the Bear River. Near Soda Springs, which struck most travelers as even more marvelous than Chimney Rock—one spring rumbled like a steamboat, and the water of another tasted like beer—Hudspeth's cutoff headed straight westward toward the Raft River, the Humboldt, and California.

All the Oregon traffic, and the rest of that headed for California, went on down the Bear, crossed to the Portneuf, and descended to Fort Hall on the Snake River. To mark the historic post, only a small stone monument survives. There is more to be learned from a replica of the fort in Pocatello's Upper Ross Park. Michael Stapleton, a history student from Idaho State University, is delighted to find someone interested in the information he is prepared to dispense. The replica and his discussion impress me with how small, and at the same time how important, was this isolated fur-trading center, supply point, and rest stop during the great days of the migration.

Nearby in the park a Mexican picnic is under way, with guitars and beer. Some of the youngsters wander over to the fort exhibits, where they display a ferocious interest in all phases of frontier Indian-killing. The irony strikes me: These Mexicans and Chicanos are at least half-Indian themselves, but they obviously feel no kinship with the Shoshones, Bannocks, and other red men of the Northwest.

Beyond the mouth of the Raft River, where the last strand for California turns off, the Oregon Trail is strictly the Oregon Trail. Still, it has its variants. One route crosses the Snake at Glenns Ferry and comes across the plains to Bonneville Point and Boise. The alternate follows the south side of the river to old Fort Boise. The united road yields one more glimpse of the Snake at Farewell Bend, then labors to the valley of the Grande Ronde, whose beauty inspired the Whitmans as they "lingered . . . for berries."

Here in the town of La Grande, Oregon, the house of the Robert Fallows sits directly on the Oregon Trail. From their backyard the ruts run back through the timber into the Blue Mountains.

The Fallows regard occupying this site as a privilege. "We feel an obligation to keep this section of the trail just as it was when we came here nearly 20 years ago," Catherine Fallow tells me. "A surprising number of people come by to see it, and we welcome them. They've all been courteous and considerate."

The accident of living squarely on the ruts of the past has given the Fallows a deeper interest in their town and region—just as Bureau of Land Management exhibits, and those of the Oregon State Parks Division, are opening the eyes of people who have lived their lives along the trail without quite realizing its significance. A rancher I find studying the ruts and reading the historical panels at Cow Hollow, south of Vale, rubs his jaw and says, "It's almost like finding out about your own family."

We probably should be surprised there's anything left to interpret and preserve. The first time I saw the ruts opposite Guernsey, Wyoming, 20 years or so ago, a crew was laying a pipeline down them. From Bonneville Point you can look along eight miles of tracks until they disappear under a new (Continued on page 74)

Bronze medallion marks one step in a 2,000-mile journey. Embedded in concrete at intervals along the trail in Wyoming, the disks salute the courageous pioneers.

"Independence Rock . . . looks like a huge whale,"
commented forty-niner J. Goldsborough Bruff
when he saw the 650-yard-long landmark.
Bruff climbed to the top to add his name to the
thousands there, and to sketch a bird's-eye view.
The artist-adventurer recorded a great variety of
events in his journal and sketchbooks. When a
buffalo (top) nearly gored a member of the group,
the cool young man avoided certain death
by chopping the enraged animal across the snout
with his bowie knife. Bruff showed his party
crossing the North Platte on a raft of cottonwood
dugouts. Not one to ignore domestic activities,
Bruff sketched a fire fueled with buffalo chips.

ABOVE: DAVID HISER; OPPOSITE: MELINDA BERGE; BELOW: PAINTING (1929) COURTESY UTAH HISTORICAL SOCIETY

The South Pass gateway

Early snow dusts the Wind River Range high above Wyoming's South Pass. The broad gap in the Rockies slopes so gradually that most wagon drivers could not tell when they crossed the Continental Divide from the Atlantic to the Pacific watershed. At left, wagons file through the pass in a William Henry Jackson painting. Their "white covers, glittering in the sunlight," looked to one imaginative 1852 observer like "ships upon the ocean." When Goldsborough Bruff in 1849 traversed the divide, he noted the "plume-formed projections" (right) that now bear the name Plume Rock.

Last lap: the Barlow Road

Etched against a September sky, Mount Hood evokes the mood of one traveler who called the peak "the grandest sight we had yet seen." At first, emigrants went to the north of Hood to raft down the surging Columbia River. In 1845 Samuel Barlow requested toll rights for a route he had marked to the south of the peak. Though safer than the river route, the Barlow Road plunged so steeply in places like Laurel Hill (opposite) that settlers had to slow their wagons with lines snubbed around trees. Some stumps still bear deep grooves burned by the ropes.

The Willamette Valley

*Misty morning breaks over Oregon's Willamette Valley,
stretching toward Mount Hood. At the British commercial
post of Fort Vancouver, opposite the mouth of the
Willamette River, the legendary Dr. John McLoughlin
welcomed thousands of newcomers to Oregon. Today
70 percent of the state's population lives in the valley,
where Perry Wells (opposite), 84, grows apples, cherries,
and prunes. Wells's grandparents followed the trail west in
1853. In 1967 Oregon bestowed on his orchard the
designation "Century Farm," given only to land owned
and worked by the same family for 100 years or more.*

subdivision that calls itself Oregon Trail Heights, thus capitalizing on what it has just effaced. Until they were finally protected by strong fences, the scratched and painted historic names at Independence Rock and Register Cliff had been all but blotted out by contemporary entries and the news that Judy loves Rick. Some of the pioneers were no better than their descendants, of course. At a dozen places along the trail, including Elm Grove, Ash Hollow, and Lone Pine in Baker Valley, emigrants calmly cut down for firewood the trees that had made campsites special. Wally Meyer ruefully rubs in the lesson when, about to leave Bonneville Point, he discovers that all his historical panels have been unbolted, ready to be carried off—perhaps to decorate some student's room, perhaps only for the curious thrill of vandalism.

For some historians, the Oregon Trail ends on the bank of the Columbia at The Dalles. But for those who believe, as I do, that it ends at Oregon City, 12 miles south of Portland, there is still one more trail experience.

The Barlow Road around Mount Hood was built in 1846 to give wagon trains an alternative to the dangerous and expensive boat trip down the Columbia to the Willamette Valley. Except in winter it is still easily passable for four-wheel-drive vehicles, and in good weather can be traversed in an ordinary car. The Forest Service has marked it with cedar posts stamped with a distinctive symbol, and has cleared underbrush from a section of the trail for hikers. Yet there are few places where one can get so vivid a sense of pathless woods and unpeopled wilderness while still driving. I follow the road from Smock Prairie, near Wamic; and for the first three hours, until I break out onto paved road near Barlow Pass, I see not a soul. Over the rocks, stumps, ruts, mud holes, creek crossings, and steep grades, I average less than six miles an hour—but still a rapid rate compared with what I could have done with an ox team.

The Willamette: This is where it truly ended, here where the land office was, in this valley where the majority of emigrants settled and where the great majority of Oregonians still live.

From here it is a long look back across distance and time to the muddy Missouri settlements of the 1830's and '40's. The history of a people, the history of a dream, the wonder of a new country are stretched out along that way. The story is of a freedom and self-reliance no longer available to us, but also of a ruthlessness and carelessness we should not want to emulate.

Yet, looking back from the cities and farms of the green Willamette Valley, across the coniferous forests of the Cascades and the Blues, across the cindery country along the Columbia and the Snake, across the memorial stillness of South Pass and down the long trough of the Platte, there is no way of thinking of the great adventure and its outcome as anything but inevitable. As long as new country with new hope lay between the settled Missouri and the beckoning Pacific, Americans were going to cross it, abuse it, seize it, settle it, and eventually come to terms with it, eventually love it as home.

Three generations of McKays harvest cauliflower—some heads weighing 15 pounds—from the land their ancestors settled near St. Paul, Oregon. James and Cecelia McKay traveled the Oregon Trail in 1847. Today the 900-acre "Century Farm" produces wheat, corn, bush beans, and strawberries as well as cauliflower.
DAVID HISER

74

Marching to Zion

By Charles McCarry

PRECEDING PAGES:
Stone figures of "This is the Place" Monument look out over environs of Salt Lake City. The sculpture commemorates the arrival of Brigham Young, President of the Church of Jesus Christ of Latter-day Saints, at the rim of the valley on July 24, 1847—ending 17 years of flight from religious persecution. Seemingly lost in a vision of the future, Young finally exclaimed: "It is enough! This is the right place."

The day began with a prayer, as all things do for the Mormons. Then the sun rose and the wagons rolled.

At the start there was brief confusion, for this was the first day of the journey westward. A pair of sturdy Appaloosas, hauling a wagon up a steep slope, stumbled and fell in a tangle of harness. Mothers anxiously counted the children whose towheads would be the company's bright guidons across a wilderness marked only by the faintest of wagon tracks.

But by midday the caravan—eight covered wagons and some 50 men, women, and children—was strung out in good order over the high plain. Dust billowed from front wagon to back. Teamsters drew bandannas over their noses and mouths while the long-skirted women beside them pinched shut the wings of their sunbonnets. Cooking pots ringing like cymbals with the sway of the wagons, the squeak of axles, the nicker of a horse recognizing a friend, the last words of a joke and its echo of laughter—these were the music of the trail.

The wagon train covered 23 miles the first day, a prodigious distance. There was a fine supper of beef and scalloped potatoes and corn and apple pie, cooked in iron Dutch ovens buried in heaps of coals raked from the fiercely burning campfire of juniper logs. Afterward a pretty little girl sang a song about the Mormon Trail, and Joe Bolander, the patriarch of the company, told stories of the harsh

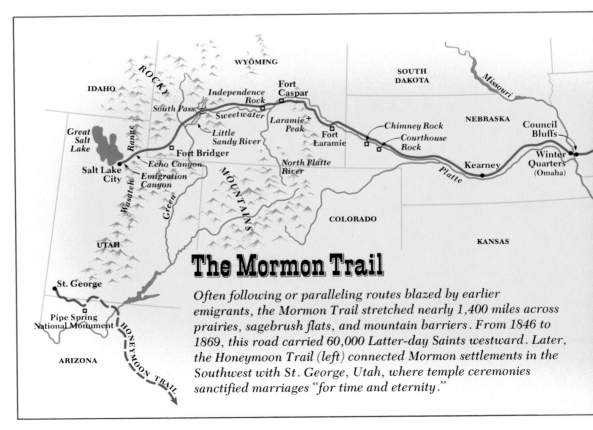

The Mormon Trail

Often following or paralleling routes blazed by earlier emigrants, the Mormon Trail stretched nearly 1,400 miles across prairies, sagebrush flats, and mountain barriers. From 1846 to 1869, this road carried 60,000 Latter-day Saints westward. Later, the Honeymoon Trail (left) connected Mormon settlements in the Southwest with St. George, Utah, where temple ceremonies sanctified marriages "for time and eternity."

country ahead. "It's dust and wind and alone, and no live water sometimes for a hundred miles." His gentle voice carried across the fire circle. "You can farm it all right, but you've got to hold your foot on the seed till it sprouts or it'll blow away on you."

The travelers went to their bedrolls early, and as they settled down under a canopy of stars, the camp was filled with the murmur of prayer. Some, as they drifted off to sleep, may have wondered which of the stars was Kolob, the heavenly body Mormons believe is closest to the throne of God. . . .

The time was not—as may have been assumed—the 19th century. It was, in fact, September 1978, and my wife, Nancy, and I were celebrating our 25th wedding anniversary on an old Mormon trace called the Honeymoon Trail. We had started out—Nancy on the high seat of a wagon, I on a mild-mannered piebald—from Pipe Spring National Monument, on the Kaibab Paiute Indian Reservation in Arizona. Our four-day trip would take us more than 70 miles across the high desert of the Arizona Strip to the temple of the Church of Jesus Christ of Latter-day Saints at St. George, in Utah's southwestern corner. Among our companions on the trail were many descendants of Mormons who had passed this way three or four generations before, to be "sealed" in marriage at the temple "for time and eternity," according to the rituals of their faith.

Just before dawn, Nancy and I woke. We had the haunting feeling, as we looked around at the dark shapes of the wagons drawn up in a circle, that we had gone to sleep in one century and wakened in another. Twenty feet away a campfire leapt in the darkness, silhouetting the figures of men in slouch hats. Out beyond, a coyote howled. Nancy had never heard that mournful sound before.

"Look," she said, as a wondering smile lit her face. Between the coyote's howl and its next breath, the sky had filled from horizon to horizon with a dawn as red as the campfire's flames. "How beautiful!" cried my wife. But minutes later, as we lined up with our plates for breakfast, a pelting rain driven by a south wind dropped sizzling into the Dutch ovens. The driver of Nancy's wagon, a sandy-haired frontiersman (and civil engineer in everyday life) named Don Marchant, offered his compliments to the chef. "The cook got the taters just right," said Don. "It's hard to get exactly the right amount of sand in them when it's rainin' this hard."

That set exactly the right note of cheerfulness, and we hitched up and saddled up and bundled up and rolled on in the downpour. It was 20 miles to our next campground.

I tied my piebald to a tailgate and rode part way with Mel Heaton, driver of the Appaloosas, who was also the organizer of this trek along the Honeymoon Trail. "It hasn't rained in this country for more than a hundred days, not a drop," said Mel, white teeth grinning through a stubble of beard, a bead of moisture on every bristle. "It sure beats the dust." Mel looked on the rain as a blessing. And so would all of us, Mormon and "gentile" alike, before this trip into the American past and into our American selves was over.

The rain, the dust, the "alone"—and the disappearance, if only

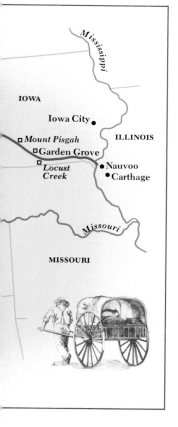

Nauvoo: memories on the Mississippi

Third-generation printer Lawrence Jones works in the restored printshop at Nauvoo while fulfilling an 18-month volunteer mission for the Mormon Church. From this shop the editors of the weekly Nauvoo Neighbor *offered subscriptions at $2 a year to the 11,000 residents of Nauvoo, one of Illinois' largest cities before the expulsion of the Mormons in 1846. Below, J. LeRoy Kimball, president of Nauvoo Restoration Inc., stands near the house of his great-grandfather, Heber C. Kimball, First Counselor to Brigham Young. Above, one of three remaining "sunstones" from the temple rests in Nauvoo State Park. Possibly representing the Celestial Kingdom, it serves as a mute reminder of the Mormon heritage.*

for a few days, of our own times as if they had dropped behind the barren painted mountains that were our landmarks—taught us more than we knew we had to learn.

Weeks later, in the neat living room of the late Paul Henderson and his wife, Helen, in Bridgeport, Nebraska, Mrs. Henderson told me a story that touched chords of memory and legend. The couple had devoted a lifetime to exploring the emigrant trails and their lore, and Mrs. Henderson's anecdote had to do with mirages—those mysterious pictures in the air that were seen by travelers across the plains. "Seventy years ago my uncle, just a boy, was coming home from milking, and he looked up," she said. "There was a covered wagon going along in the sky, the bowed top, the driver and his wife perched there, the oxen. There was even a dog trotting behind. The real wagon may have been 15, 20 miles away."

By the time I met the Hendersons I was already well on the way to completing my journey on the Mormon Trail. In the end, I covered every foot of it that could be found—by highway where it

Quitting Nauvoo, refugee wagons cross the icy Mississippi River on flatboats and enter Iowa. Although the Mormons had agreed to leave "as soon as grass grows and water runs," increasing tension between them and state officials prompted the Saints to start their exodus in February 1846. Soon a providential freezing of the Mississippi permitted wagons to cross on the ice—dramatically reminding the faithful of an earlier exodus and the parting of the Red Sea before the tribes of Israel.

follows highway, by compass and map and often by gosh and by golly in the many places where it passes through open country, its ruts still visible to the educated eye.

I took a pair of highly educated eyes along with me—not my own, but those of Professor Stanley B. Kimball, an expert on the Mormon Trail and a great-great-grandson of Heber C. Kimball. Along with Joseph Smith, prophet and founder of the Church of Jesus Christ of Latter-day Saints, and Brigham Young, its second president, Heber Kimball was one of the three most important figures in the early church. The incumbent president of the church, Spencer W. Kimball, is likewise a direct descendant of Heber.

"Like most Mormons, I am rich in cousins," Stanley Kimball told me. "My great-great-grandfather had 43 wives and 65 children. Only 17 of the wives were 'conjugal'; with the others he had just a protective relationship. Otherwise we'd have a worse job of sorting each other out at family reunions than we do now."

From 1846 to 1869 about 60,000 Mormon pioneers, from the American states then existing and from many countries in Europe, crossed the prairies. These converts to a new religion had earlier

Right: Mormons pulling handcarts ford a stream and pause to rest, as curious Indians approach on horseback. Handcart companies, first organized in 1856 by Brigham Young to move impoverished European converts westward from Iowa City, persevered despite exhaustion, malnutrition, hostile weather, and frequent breakdowns. Winter caught two companies still on the trail, and 200 people died. The artist who painted these four pictures, C.C.A. Christensen, himself traveled to Utah as a young man hauling a handcart.

Exodus of the Saints

Forged in adversity, the Mormon migration ranks high among the achievements of America's westward expansion. At left, "mobbers" force Saints from Jackson County, Missouri, in 1833. At far left, church founder Joseph Smith, in the uniform of a lieutenant general, inspects the Nauvoo Legion. Formed to protect the Mormon community, the 4,000-member legion aggravated mistrust among the citizens of Illinois. Driven from Nauvoo, the refugees established Winter Quarters (below, left) on the Missouri River where a suburb of Omaha, Nebraska, now stands. Hundreds perished here while the Saints waited for spring.

been driven out of Ohio and Missouri by neighbors suspicious of their faith, fearful of their political power, and perhaps envious of their prosperity. The beehive is a favorite symbol of the industrious Mormons, and wherever they have gone they have taken land that no one else thought useful and made it, in the biblical phrase loved by Brigham Young, "blossom as the rose."

After fleeing from Missouri in 1838-39, the followers of Joseph Smith purchased a large tract of malarial swamp on the Illinois bank of the Mississippi River and built what Mormons still call "Nauvoo the Beautiful."

Smith, born on a farm in Sharon, Vermont, in 1805, had moved with his family to another farm near Palmyra, New York. There, he said, an angel delivered to him a set of golden plates.

Joseph Smith claimed to have translated the plates by miraculous means, and in 1830 he published the resulting manuscript as the Book of Mormon. By the time Nauvoo was founded, Smith had attracted thousands of converts; and in 1844 he declared himself a candidate for President of the United States—perhaps to publicize the Mormons' failure to obtain legal protection in various states.

Then disaster struck. Growing fear of the Saints' political and economic strength in Illinois, rumors of polygamy, and finally the Mormon leaders' high-handed destruction of the *Nauvoo Expositor,* a newspaper published by dissenters, caused anti-Mormon sentiment to boil over into violent reaction. Warrants were issued for Joseph Smith's arrest on charges of riot and then of treason; and though he feared, as he told his brother Hyrum, that "we shall be butchered," he gave himself up for trial at Carthage, Illinois.

In the Carthage jail, on a soft autumn day with leaves rustling in the quiet street outside, Mrs. Dorothy Fullmer told me of the death of Joseph Smith. As she spoke, her voice trembling, I touched the bullet holes in the door of the upstairs bedroom where Joseph and Hyrum and two companions, John Taylor and Willard Richards, were being held in protective custody. "The bullets flew through the door. Hyrum Smith fell, mortally wounded. The Prophet Joseph Smith leaped to this windowsill and looked out. Below stood the Carthage Greys—the Illinois militia that had been left to protect him—content to be pushed aside by the mob surging forward, faces blackened. He cried out and jumped, or fell, pierced by bullets, to his death."

This occurred on June 27, 1844. Six weeks later Brigham Young, acting as president of the Twelve Apostles, assumed leadership of the bereaved church. "The whole state," said Governor Thomas Ford of Illinois, "is a mob." In September 1845, when violence and vigilantism on both sides had reached fever pitch, Young and other leaders of the church agreed to leave Illinois "as soon as grass grows and water runs." Actually the great migration of the Saints began in early February.

Stanley Kimball and I stood on the west bank of the Mississippi in Iowa, with the rising sun rouging the dimples on the used old face of the river. Overhead, a cloud of starlings three miles long beat westward across the morning. "You can see how hard it must have

Monarch butterflies draw nectar from sunflowers, native along much of the Mormon Trail through Iowa, Nebraska, and Wyoming.

been to leave all this," said Stanley. On the other side of the river, surrounding a spacious green, stood the neat, sturdy houses (there were more than 2,000 of them here in 1846) and the rows of trees that are the gift of a confident people to future generations. The Mormons had thought to establish Zion here, and remain forever.

On February 9, 1846, with the evacuation under way, Brigham Young looked back through the slanting light of late afternoon and saw the great white temple afire. "If it is the will of the Lord that the temple be burned, instead of being defiled by the gentiles, amen to it," said Brigham. The fire, as it turned out, was a minor one started by an overheated stovepipe; but after the Saints left, a second blaze gutted the temple, a fierce windstorm destroyed part of the walls, and finally the whole structure was razed.

The Mormons had sold what they could, at the buyers' tightfisted prices, but much was left behind unsold, including land across the river in Iowa where they had hoped to establish new communities.

In Nauvoo I talked with one of Stanley Kimball's innumerable cousins, J. LeRoy Kimball, M.D. Dr. Kimball eschews titles. Possibly the best name to put to him is "Mr. Nauvoo Restoration," for it was he who began the restoration of Nauvoo by buying Heber C. Kimball's delightful old brick manse. Later, Dr. Kimball acquired a number of other old Mormon homes, including that of Brigham Young. By now, with help from Salt Lake City, he has supervised the restoration of 14 historic buildings; a half-dozen more are in progress. I asked whether the temple, which in its time may have been the largest building in America west of the Alleghenies, would ever be rebuilt. "I believe so," said Dr. Kimball, with the smile of a man who has already seen many a dream come true. "We have the loveliest sunsets on earth here on the Mississippi. I've looked forward to the Tabernacle Choir singing here with our sunset shining on them."

Next day, as I watched the sun dapple the river, I pictured the scene as it must have been in that February 132 years before when the exodus began: a skim of snow on the black alluvial soil; bitter winds; shivering women and children; and ferries carrying the faithful and what goods were left to them across the swollen winter river, with cakes and slabs of ice swirling in the current.

The journey across Iowa was a terrible one. "Animals fed on limbs and bark of trees, as grass had not yet started," Orson Pratt wrote in his diary on March 22. Heavy rains turned the trail into a quagmire. Mud seized at the wagon wheels, and at night froze hard. Wrote Brigham's brother Lorenzo: "A gust of wind . . . blue the tent flat to the ground. . . . The rain came down in torants so fast that it put out the fire. In a few minuits it was all darkness, and it was so cold that it seemed as though I must perish."

Mormon optimism, though sorely tested, did not entirely vanish. Heber Kimball's newlywed daughter, Helen Mar Whitney, wrote, "I could . . . knit and read as we traveled, and Horace could read or play his flute. . . . [A] little wagon (Continued on page 94)

The living prairie

Impressed by the abundance and variety of prairie wildlife, the Saints studied
as well as hunted the animals they encountered. Today the land still supports many
creatures. Above, curious pronghorns survey their surroundings. Below,
a burrowing owl peers from its den; a greater prairie chicken begins its courtship
dance. Opposite, a solitary black-eyed Susan flickers in a field of blazing star.
From the frontier, Mormon leaders wrote their followers to expect "rolling prairies
. . . decorated with a growth of flowers so gorgeous . . . as to exceed description."

Wasatch Range, here ablaze with autumn, offers scenes "truly wild and melancholy," reported

GORDON BEALL

William Clayton in 1847. The emigrants found the final miles "steep, lengthy and tedious."

Brigham Young, second
president of the LDS
Church, proved an
adroit and forceful
administrator in
directing the
migration of the Saints
and their resettlement.
Territorial governor
from 1850 to 1857, he
continued in effect to
rule the people of
Utah from his church
post until his death
in 1877.

all to ourselves, which, under the circumstances, was next thing to paradise." The Nauvoo Brass Band played at night for the shivering Saints; and how that music, issuing from instruments licked by the firelight, must have quivered with memories of happier nights!

Little trace is left here of the progress of the Camp of Israel, as the Mormons in their flight styled themselves. Famous camp-grounds in the Mormon legend are plain fields, crossed by mild creeks with willows nodding on the banks.

The Camp of Israel, after considerable disorder at the outset, became probably the best organized migration in American history. Formed into companies of one hundred families, each under a captain, every wagon train was supported by the skills of artisans—blacksmiths, carpenters, and so on. Each woman was a cook and seamstress. Each man was a herdsman or farmer, and, when need arose, a soldier. The camp marched under the discipline of faith, and Brigham Young, as its Moses and its commanding general, issued prayers, exhortations, or reprimands as circumstances required.

The progress west through Iowa in 1846 was, for the Saints as for all who passed this way, a matter of crossing rivers. Locust Creek, just east of the modern-day town of Sewal, Iowa, is surely the most famous stream in Mormon history. Here William Clayton, official clerk of the exodus and strong right arm to Brigham all his life, wrote the words of the hymn that most deeply stirs Mormon hearts—"Come, Come Ye Saints." Clayton, accompanied by three of his wives, had left another, Diantha, in Nauvoo, great with child. On Wednesday, April 15, news came to Clayton that Diantha, though sick with ague and mumps, had given birth to a son 15 days earlier. That same morning, he recorded, "I composed a new song—'All is Well.'" Those were the last words of the hymn, and they became the marching motto of the Saints.

A few miles beyond, at Garden Grove, the Camp of Israel established its first real way station. Showing characteristic diligence, the Saints, with more than 170 men working, cleared 715 acres in three weeks, cut 10,000 rails for fences, built houses. This was to be a place to offer shelter and succor for those coming behind—and that was the keynote of the western movement of the Mormons. All along the trail, they built and planted and improved, cut down steep river-banks and constructed ferries, signposted exact distances, and set up storehouses of food and other supplies. They knew that their faith would beckon thousands across the prairies, and that what they accomplished would make the journey easier for those who followed.

Beyond Garden Grove lies Mount Pisgah, so named by one of Brigham's stalwarts, Parley P. Pratt, for the biblical upland. It was, when we mounted this little rise in the prairie, a mild day, with the distances of America lying to the west under the soft light of a yellow sun. Yet a sharp wind blew, cold as the air that rises from marble. Here, in the first six months of 1846, bedded sometimes in caves, an estimated 150 pioneers died of the scourges of the trail—black scurvy, cholera, typhoid, tuberculosis—or in childbirth. Before the site was abandoned in 1852, perhaps as many as 800 died here.

Revered survivors of the Pioneers of 1847 assemble in Salt Lake City on Pioneer Day, 1905. Below, two of Brigham Young's granddaughters—Naomi Schettler, right, with representatives of four more generations of her family, and Gladys Orlob, with three—meet for a group portrait in Young's Beehive House. Brigham had at least 27 wives and 57 children; his descendants number in the thousands.

Even greater suffering was yet to come. The Saints crossed the Missouri River at Council Bluffs, and set up a new camp on Indian lands. This encampment on the Missouri, at what is now the Omaha suburb of Florence, Nebraska, became known as Winter Quarters. A memorial plaque in the Mormon Pioneer Cemetery says that of the 3,483 Saints who wintered here in dugouts, sod houses, and rude log cabins, more than 600 died of fever and other ailments. Neither the medicaments of the time nor the laying on of hands, a common means of healing among the Mormons, availed against the epidemic. Love was the ultimate therapy. As Patty Sessions, one of the midwives, lay gravely ill, Brigham Young came to her. To the women nursing her he said, "You must all hold on to her as long as she breathes." In this case love worked its miracle. Mrs. Sessions recovered and lived to the age of 98.

As spring approached, perhaps 10,000 Mormons were encamped on both sides of the Missouri River, about 3,500 in Winter Quarters and the remainder at Mount Pisgah, Garden Grove, and Council Bluffs in Iowa or scattered along the trail, working to raise money for the Camp of Israel.

Recognizing that it was impossible even for so well organized a people as the Saints to move such a large number in one body, Brigham Young and the Council of the Twelve determined that a pioneer company should be sent ahead to mark the trail, measure the hazards, and—highest of objectives—lay the cornerstone of the new Zion. Brigham knew that he was heading for the valley of the Great Salt Lake, and he had maps of a sort, but few had ever actually seen that empty desert.

With biblical sonority he announced that the First Pioneer Company would consist only of vigorous males. But Brigham, if he was a stern man, was also a man with a most human weakness—he loved his brother Lorenzo, and he couldn't find it in his heart to refuse Lorenzo's plea to take along his ailing wife Harriet and her two children. Brigham then decided to bring one of his own wives, Harriet's daughter Clara, and Heber Kimball brought one as well—Ellen Sanders. When the expedition started west on April 5, 1847, it numbered 144 men and boys, three women, and two children. There were 72 wagons, 93 horses, 52 mules, 66 oxen, 19 cows, and 17 dogs.

Wilford Woodruff, later to be the church president who, in 1890, suspended the practice of polygamy, had prepared soberly for the journey. "I have never felt more wait upon my mind . . . while leaving my family to go on a mission than now," he wrote in his diary.

On April 18, reports Woodruff, "President Young called the captains together [14 men including Woodruff, one for every ten Saints in the company] and gave them instructions to travel in the morning two abreast & let all who were not driving teams carry their guns [capped and loaded] & walk by the side of the waggons, let no man go away hunting to get out of sight of the camp. The bugle was to be blown at half-past 7 o'clock at night when all was to go to prayer in their several waggons and retire to bed. . . . The Bugle will blow at 5 o'clock in the morning & two hours will be allotted to the camp to arise & pray, breakfast, feed horses, harness, and start at the blowing of the bugle at 7 o'clock."

Stanley Kimball and I, striking west from Winter Quarters into Nebraska, traveled through a landscape of fertile fields, with neat white houses scattered among them and innumerable clumps of trees breaking up the monotony of a seemingly endless land. But in 1847, as Paul Henderson once explained to me, there were scarcely two trees between Grand Island and Fort Laramie, a distance of more than 300 miles. Among the rare signs of humanity were the occasional Indians who appeared on the horizon—and sometimes ventured closer. But for the whole 111 days of their trip to the Salt Lake Valley, Brigham's men had no real trouble with the Indians. "Perhaps the pioneers realized," Stanley Kimball said, "that Indians who were usually described as 'thieves' by white men passing through their territory were, in truth, toll collectors. That was a concept Brigham Young would have understood, and approved."

As Stanley spoke, we were standing on a broad plain where, on May 1, the pioneers had their first buffalo hunt. It was a wild affair, with Mormon horsemen more than once in peril of being tumbled by the great beasts. Heber Kimball borrowed a 15-shooter and joined the rest. Stanley, in his mind's eye, watched in amusement as his great-great-grandfather, dropped reins trailing while he aimed the big rifle, galloped precariously in phantom dust among phantom beasts. Twelve buffalo were killed, and the Saints feasted.

The teeming game—they saw antelope and wolves and myriad birds as well as bison—was a temptation, and on May 18, Brigham Young "sharply reproved the hunters for shooting so much meat when it was not needed."

The company had by this time crossed the 100th meridian, which lies near the present-day town of Cozad, Nebraska. West of this line there is insufficient rainfall to grow unirrigated crops, and there the imaginative traveler can scent the parched wind of "the great American desert."

If the Mormons did not know what a fateful line they had crossed, they nevertheless missed few landmarks and few natural phenomena. Their man of science, Orson Pratt, took daily measurements with barometer and compass; and part way across Nebraska the company's jack-of-all-trades, Appleton Harmon, installed a remarkable device designed by Pratt and William Clayton that was activated by a screw and a wheel of 60 cogs and measured mileage. They called it a "roadometer"; mounted on a wagon wheel, it provided an accurate measure of elapsed distance on the way west.

When the Mormons reached the site of present-day Kearney, Nebraska, they remained on the north bank of the Platte River, and this is what distinguishes the Mormon Trail from the Oregon Trail in this section: The latter ran along the south bank. The Mormons chose the north side not so much to isolate themselves across the shallow stream as to avoid competing for grazing and campsites. From here it was 300 miles to Fort Laramie along a broad, flat floodplain, a natural highway running between low bluffs. The Platte was a godsend, for it provided water and forage and easy passage. If it hadn't been there, the United States might well have ended at the mighty Missouri.

Near today's town of Sutherland, the company entered Nebraska's sandhill country. Stanley and I, early one morning, climbed a hill his forebears had dubbed "the ox killer." The slope seemed gentle enough, but when we reached the top with the Platte glittering far below, and looked to the east at a field dotted with minute haystacks and tiny Angus cattle, I realized just why it had been named. The lowing of the cattle was a reminder of the suffering of the oxen that had labored up this hill with the yoke biting their necks and sand clutching at their hooves.

A few miles farther on, we found ourselves in the dooryard of Stan Schutte, who was up early doing some weekend carpentry. According to our maps, the trail passed right by his house. "Hold this," said Stan, handing me a large post he'd been fitting as a support to the corner of his garage. He went indoors and came out with a deed that showed the exact location of the trail, not 15 feet from his front step. "Do you," I asked, "ever hear the ghostly creak of Conestogas in the night?" Stan grinned. "Nope. You're in *Nebraska*, mister—the wind drowns *everything* out!"

From Indian Lookout, west of Lisco, Porter Rockwell excited the Mormons by a report that he had seen Chimney Rock—estimated from rough maps to be halfway to the Salt Lake. Stanley Kimball and I tried with eight-power glasses but could glimpse neither this famous landmark nor its companions, Courthouse Rock and Jail Rock.

By now it was late May, and the pioneers, gradually growing accustomed to the routine of the trail, were finding ways to amuse themselves after long days of slow walking and hard work. Music and dancing have always been part of the Mormon way of life; but on May 28 a lively dance and musicale, joined by the three black slaves who accompanied the pioneer company, had gone on too long. The next morning Brigham assembled the company, mounted a wagon, and issued one of the tongue-lashings for which he was to be as famous in his lifetime as for his piousness and his political wisdom. According to Woodruff's diary, Brigham thundered: ". . . I would rather be alone & I am now resolved not to go any further with this camp unless you . . . quit your folley and wickedness. Nearly the whole camp has been card playing & dancing & Nigaring & hoaring. . . . O yes, you did play cards, dice, checkers, & dominoes! . . . You would shrink from the glance of the eyes of God's angels!"

The rest of the day the chastened company proceeded in a marked change of mood, and the next—May 30, a Sabbath—was set aside as a day of prayer and fasting. After a morning prayer meeting, Brigham and the other Apostles donned their temple robes—"about as solemn a thing as you could possibly do," explains Stanley—and retired to pray and meditate.

Two days later they camped on the south side of the Platte near Fort Laramie. Here a grand reunion was held, for they met a party of

Mormons, led by the Robert Crow family, who had come up from Mississippi and wintered at Pueblo, Colorado. They were 543¼ miles from Winter Quarters, and about to say goodbye to the Platte.

Stanley and I, crossing into Wyoming, caught our first glimpse of Laramie Peak, a blue pyramid, first wandering child of what Stanley and his forebears called "the sure-'nuff Rockies." We stopped to ask a courteous farmer named Albert Fisher for directions to the trail. "Go west," he advised, "and you'll see ruts—they're blowed out 20 feet deep. You'll see 'em, all right!"

We did, and the sight sent Stanley's blood coursing. "This is Mexican Hill! They all groaned and had a fit about Mexican Hill!" It was a dizzying slope carved through sandstone by thousands of wagon wheels.

Stanley leaped into our four-wheel-drive vehicle and plunged down the steep chute. At the bottom, he looked upward in glee. "I'll bet no Mormon has gone down that since pioneer times."

We set out cross-country, and despite the formidable roll of large-scale maps Stanley had brought along, we soon found ourselves hopelessly lost near Medicine Bow National Forest. If one must be lost, one couldn't pick a better place—we were just north of the 42nd parallel at 5,300 feet, not far from Horseshoe Creek, with Squaw Peaks and Elk, Rock, and Black mountains breaking the horizon. Following a pair of ruts through sagebrush, we came upon Coffee Creek, and saw in the distance—most unexpected of sights—a large Tudor house. There seemed to be nobody home except three skittish fat chestnuts with their manes and tails filled with burdocks.

Then a bucketing pickup splashed through the creek, and a young fellow named A. L. Gruwell jumped out. He showed us the trail and the way out, making that cheery gift of valuable time and natural trust that is the mark of the man close to the western land.

As we drove out we passed through a stand of aspens, bright gold in the crisp September afternoon. "No pioneer ever saw aspens golden in Wyoming and lived to see Oregon," Stanley said. Turning leaves on the Laramie range meant snow, and snow meant death.

At Fort Caspar, where the Mormons built a famous ferry across the last horseshoe of the Platte (no trace of the old ferry remains), Stanley and I moved along the trail past beds of saleratus, a natural baking soda. "They were pleased with themselves when it made bread rise," said Stanley. "They also washed their hair in sagebrush—it made the scalp tingle—and drank so much of an herbal brew that it's still known to some as 'Mormon tea.' "

We climbed the long hill called Poison Spider Road and passed through Emigrant Gap, so mild a gateway to the west that one would not know he was there unless he had been told. All around us, shy and curious and utterly unafraid, antelope played. We rolled down the window and said hello. They leaped away, yellow and black and white, pretty as ballerinas. It wasn't fear, I thought, that made them run, but pride in their loveliness.

A rifle-shot west of Independence Rock, a hump of soft stone covered by the carved initials of pioneers *(Continued on page 104)*

The Honeymoon Trail

Present-day pilgrims relive some of the 50-year history of the Honeymoon Trail in a four-day, 70-mile journey by wagon train from Pipe Spring, Arizona, to St. George, Utah. Before completion of an Arizona temple at Mesa in 1929, Mormon newlyweds from Arizona and New Mexico followed this route to reach the St. George temple for the "sealing" of their marriages. In the time exposure above, early risers ring a roaring campfire before beginning another ten-hour day on the trail. Above, right, David Finicum steadies a wagon yoke on a rocky stretch along Utah's Hurricane Fault.

and, unfortunately, by those of much more recent travelers, we came upon a grim reminder of death in the snow. Martins Cove is a name solemn in Mormon folklore. Here in November 1856, the 576 members of Handcart Company No. 4, led by Captain Edward Martin, were trapped by an early blizzard. They had walked across the plains, trundling all their belongings in high-wheeled carts. Though a rescue party from Salt Lake City reached them, 145 died here.

Stanley Kimball and I went far back into the pocket in the hills where so many suffered in this silent hiding place. To the east rose castellated gray rocks, stained by some faded pink mineral. In the rustling timothy were beds where deer had lain the night before, and we saw two mule-deer does, then a band of five white-tails bounding up the steep rocks among juniper and spruce. The cove is invisible from a distance of a hundred yards. Somewhere in this ground, in unmarked graves, lie the dead. In the air was the smell of snow.

Next to the Platte, the most important stream on the trail is the Sweetwater, which washes the base of Independence Rock and then meanders across the trail in many fordings for the next 93 miles. The Sweetwater has its great moment when it plunges through Devils Gate, a massive split rock 370 feet high just east of Martins Cove and west of Independence Rock. Then it becomes a whispering brook, humble, hardly noticeable—but lifter of the cup of life to all who passed through this thirsty country to the mountains.

Farther to the west, just short of the Continental Divide, we came upon the ghost of a ranch house, ready to fall from fatigue as it leaned into the curve of time. Beyond we found the Strawberry, a shining creek in a gemlike meadow. Nothing in the records suggests that Mormons ever camped here, but Stanley and I agreed that they should have. We found our way out, with a full moon shining in the last daylight in the east, and the sun burning bright in the west.

On June 28, at the Little Sandy some miles west of the divide, the pioneers met Jim Bridger, most famous of the mountain men— and, with good fortune that must have seemed divinely inspired to the Mormons, one of the few white men who had seen the Salt Lake Valley. His trading post, Fort Bridger, was a hundred miles to the southwest. He spent the night in camp, yarning until well past the Saints' bedtime, giving Brigham and the others all manner of information and encouragement. He did wonder if wheat and corn would grow in the valley, considering the coldness of the nights.

At Fort Bridger, the Mormon Trail diverged from that of the others that went west. The Oregonians and Californians turned north. The Mormons turned south and west toward the fanged Wasatch Range.

On June 30, while encamped on the banks of the Green River among wild apple trees and wild roses, Brigham's men were joined by Samuel Brannan, a Mormon who had left New York by ship on February 4, 1846. He and his company had sailed around Cape Horn and founded a Mormon colony on San Francisco Bay. He sang the praises of the California climate, but Brigham would hear none of it:

PRECEDING PAGES: Strong arms heave an errant wagon back onto the trail along the Rock Canyon dugway—a 1,500-foot descent to the floor of Warner Valley, Utah.

Spirits undampened by a downpour, Nancy McCarry, the author's wife, warms herself before a breakfast campfire. "An altogether incredible trip," she reported. "I can't think of a more memorable way to spend a 25th wedding anniversary!"

DAVID HISER;
PRECEDING PAGES: MELINDA BERGE

104

He was leading the Saints to sanctuary; they would make their own paradise in the desert—perhaps, even, their own country.

In subsequent years, patriotism was instilled in every Mormon, but the times in which these fugitives fled were times of disillusion with a government that had done so little to protect them in the free practice of their religion. On July 4 one of Brigham's company, Norton Jacob, wrote in his journal: "This is Uncle Sam's day of Independence, well we are independent of all the powers of the Gentiles and that's enough for us."

Like many others in the company, Jacob, as he wrote, lay ill with a malady the pioneers called "mountain fever." Historians speculate this may have been either Rocky Mountain spotted fever or Colorado tick fever, both carried by wood ticks. It was excruciating, with pains in the joints and headache and fever, and sometimes delirium; but the sickness was not fatal, and it passed after a few days.

By the time Norton Jacob was stricken, the pioneer company was only about a hundred miles from its goal. But these would be the most difficult miles of the journey. On July 12 Brigham Young himself was stricken with mountain fever. Evidently he had a particularly bad case, for Brigham, the Lion of the Lord, was unable to rise from his pallet. Still, he was not too sick to keep the Saints to their labor. A party was sent ahead to build a road through the mountains. At these higher elevations, water froze in the buckets at night even in July; the men found snow in the shade and had a snowball fight. But elder was in flower, gooseberries were ripe, and—prophecy of fertility—wild roses and wild wheat and other alpine flora bloomed by the banks of clean rushing streams and pure springs. The mountains glittered with minerals.

The work party slashed at tangles of willow, manhandled rock, laid crude road. The wagons, mile by painful mile, came on. Willow stubble slashed the hooves of oxen and horses. One man's wagon, with two children inside, overturned, but fortunately there were no injuries.

The Mormons passed through Echo Canyon, over Big Mountain and Little Mountain and down Emigration Canyon, and then—on July 24, 1847—Brigham Young came into full view of the valley of the Great Salt Lake. Still feverish and weak, he was lying in Wilford Woodruff's carriage, and he lifted himself to look down on the promised destination. Many years afterward Woodruff was to recall that Brigham at that moment said, "It is enough. This is the right place." It has often been remarked that if Brigham Young did not actually say that, he should have. What Woodruff himself said, on the very day

At St. George the trek participants, including Jay and Karen Findlay, assemble for a presentation to temple officials of produce and dairy products from Pipe Spring.

MELINDA BERGE

as recorded in his journal, expresses the soaring song in his heart:

". . . land of promise, held in reserve by the hand of GOD for a resting place for the Saints . . . our hearts were surely made glad . . . to gaze upon a valley of such vast extent entirely surrounded with a perfect chain of everlasting hills & mountains covered with the eternal snows . . . towering toward Heaven."

Others had come down into the valley two days before them. Five acres of land had already been put under irrigation, and a crop was in the ground. Tradition says that Brigham thrust his cane into the soil and selected a site for the temple. "And we will have a city clean and in order," he decreed.

And so, ever since, they have, with the everlasting hills and mountains covered with snow towering toward Heaven.

Six generations later, Nancy and I, a pair of gentiles, stood by a campfire in a driving rain, soaked to the skin and blissfully happy. We were encamped on the rim of Hurricane Fault in the high country along the Utah-Arizona border. Magically, musical instruments appeared. Amusing songs of the trail were sung—and all of us suddenly realized that these simple ditties had a practical purpose: to drive the chill from your bones and the hopelessness from your heart. "We want a bear story!" several cried, and Owen Johnson, our wagon master, told one. We went to bed. Rain poured through the canvas of our tent, and the hobbled horses stumbled through camp, crashing into the chuck wagon with a clatter of pots.

Next day, Mel Heaton and his men took our wagons down the face of Hurricane Fault—a drop of 1,500 feet in less than a mile. There were whoops and hurrahs, but no accidents, though no man now alive had taken wagons down this dugway, hardly as wide as the span of the axle, until Mel and Joe Bolander did it three years ago.

We had one last camp, and dried our clothes and sleeping bags in the sun that shone on us at last. I spoke to Bill Gold, of Phoenix, whose wife is a descendant of one of the Honeymoon Trail marriages. "I'm glad we had the rain," I said. Bill agreed—but it was no surprise to him, raised on tales of Mormon persecution and Mormon heroism and safe in his Mormon faith, that misfortune is a balm, not a wound.

Next day we approached St. George, and in the distance saw its temple, white as salt. We were met at the gates of the temple by a group of dignitaries. Adeline Johnson presented a gift of produce and homemade cheese from the ranch at Pipe Spring to the temple president with modest blushes and—I thought—the hint of a tear behind her glasses.

Her husband, Owen, said, "Someone asked me why I travel in this wagon train. We just like to get back into that time where our fathers are, and on that old, rough trail."

Said Temple President Grant T. Bowler to Mel Heaton, "Truly are we grateful to you, Brother Heaton, for keeping alive this tradition. I hope you'll keep it up."

Mel, dusty hat in hand, beard stubbly, replied, "You bet!"

How else would a pioneer cry "Amen!"?

Teamster Orval Palmer muses over the last day's ride. A rancher from Alton, Utah, Palmer and other cowboys added realism to the adventure for the trail group's city-bred greenhorns. For Palmer, the Pipe Spring Wagon Trek meant an opportunity to sample the experience of his parents, who traveled to St. George as honeymooners in 1919.

DAVID HISER

To the Rainbow's End
By Robert Laxalt

LITHOGRAPH BY N. CURRIER, 1849; COURTESY THE OAKLAND MUSEUM HISTORY DEPARTMENT

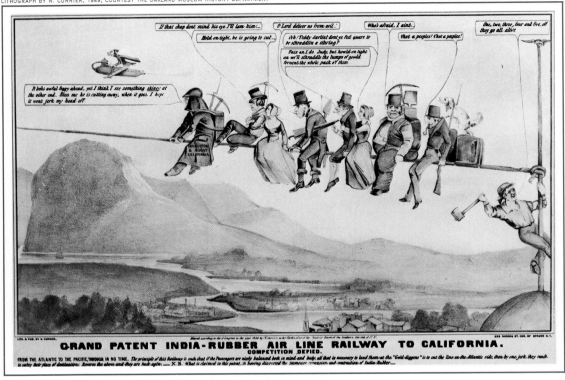

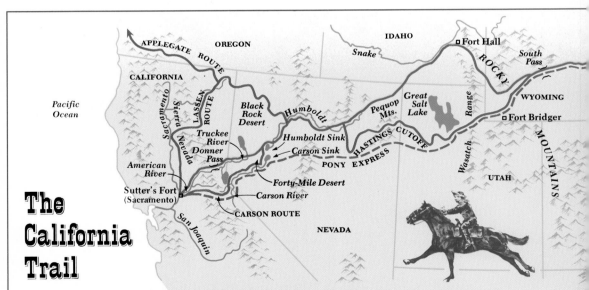

The California Trail

Following the Oregon Trail from the Missouri River to South Pass, emigrants bound for California then branched out—some north of the Great Salt Lake, others south, before seeking out the Humboldt River "lifeline." On the desert approaches to the Sierra Nevada, routes again diverged; but all forced travelers to face risks and endure severe hardships.

Now came the crucible. Now was the time when the pioneers' mettle would be tested in the furnace heat of deserts and tempered in the freezing cold of the Sierra Nevada, the last barrier between them and their promised land: California.

Behind lay 1,200 miles and three months of mostly prairie travel along the Oregon Trail from the outposts of civilization on the Missouri River. By the time they reached the departure points to California—just west of South Pass on the Continental Divide in Wyoming, or near Fort Hall in Idaho—the trail had already taken a heavy toll. Weary humans and exhausted oxen and mules were ill prepared for what was to come.

Even in their worst imaginings, the emigrants could not suspect what was in store over the next 800 miles: the remaining challenges of the rugged Rockies; then weeks of plodding through loose sand; days of little or no water; nights of vigilance against thieving, sometimes hostile Indians; the backbreaking toil of hauling wagons across some 70 miles of the Sierra, haunted by the fear of early snows.

Some would take the ordeal in stride; some later would even romanticize it; some would rise to the finest heights of heroism; some would descend to avarice and brutality; a few would be driven to cannibalism; and the characters of all would be marked forever.

This was the California Trail—or, more accurately, a network of proven routes and misleading "shortcuts," the latter laid out by scheming empire builders to lure settlers to their own California domains. In the dozen years that began with 1846, more than 165,000 pioneers made the crossing.

I penetrated that network of trails through blazing midsummer deserts to the first winter snows in the Sierra Nevada, seeking my own measure of what the pioneers of a century and more ago had endured. It was a sobering, humbling experience.

As with other trails west, the California Trail was opened by spasmodic thrusts into the unknown.

The most important stretch of what was to become the main California Trail was the path of the Humboldt River. Flowing sinuously from northeastern Nevada some 400 miles across the arid flatlands lying between mountain ranges of the Great Basin, this lifeline provided the water and grass so vital to the emigrant trains.

Nearly two decades after the original scouting of the region by the mountain men, the Bartleson-Bidwell party became in 1841 the first group of emigrants to try to open a wagon trail across Nevada to California. It was a haphazard, blundering adventure through an uncharted wilderness. Long before reaching the Sierra, the struggling travelers had to abandon their wagons. But even finishing on a pack trail served to prove that the 2,000-mile journey to California was possible. A California Trail was open, though only half was wagon road, and much was never used again.

The party was an incongruous mixture of 31 young men, one woman and her infant daughter, and nine meagerly provisioned wagons drawn by oxen and mules. The motives for the journey were just as mixed: escape from economic depression that gripped the East, flight from the ravages of cholera and malaria, heady tales of land for the taking in California, and plain westering adventure.

The Bartleson-Bidwell party followed the Oregon Trail as far as Soda Springs, Idaho, turned southward and dipped into northwest Utah, then entered eastern Nevada. At the base of the Pequop Mountains they were forced to leave the last of their wagons. Guided only by stories passed by word of mouth, they searched frantically for the Humboldt River lifeline, finally found it, and followed it to its sink. But ahead, still between them and the Sierra, lay a waterless wasteland that was to become notorious as the Forty-Mile Desert.

The ordeal seemed endless. The entire party very nearly perished from starvation and lack of water. In the desert they began killing their oxen for food. Once in the Sierra they found abundant water but little game. Crossing the summit at Sonora Pass, they stumbled into the maze of canyons of the Stanislaus River. After their last ox, they ate mule meat until at last they reached the lush, game-filled San Joaquin Valley on October 30, 1841. The young woman, Nancy Kelsey, walked barefoot into Marsh's Ranch, carrying her baby.

The route of the Bartleson-Bidwell party and later emigrant trains down the Humboldt River has been traced and marked in recent years by Trails West, a group of some 125 members interested in frontier history, and by the Nevada Emigrant Trail Marking Committee. I joined several Trails West representatives in the deserts of northern Nevada in early August, when temperatures were soaring above 100. Their task is not an easy one, even in these sparsely settled regions. "Washouts and erosion have erased big chunks of the trails," Marshall Guisti, president of Trails West, told me. "And what was once open country along the routes is being fenced off, more each year, so permission to pass becomes a big problem."

When we parted company, I set off to follow the winding Humboldt River to its sink about 20 miles south of present-day Lovelock. Along the way, I turned off Interstate Highway 80 and ventured into the blistered sagebrush desert on foot. Vast tablelands and drab mountains stretched into interminable distance. Here and there, several of the furious whirlwinds called dust devils boiled up from the desert floor and went twisting away.

As I walked I tried to imagine the sufferings of the pioneers. The vast dome of the sky was a hot, burning blue, the sun a relentless, blinding orb. There was not a tree anywhere, and I imagined the yearning of the pioneers for one tiny bit of shade. The shimmering desert seemed to suck the moisture out of my body. In the afternoon a breeze sprang up, but it brought no relief: The eddies of air were like gusts from a blast furnace. I began to imagine the pioneers' state of mind as they realized that the worst was yet to come.

From the last poor water and grass at the sink of the Humboldt River, the Forty-Mile Desert begins—an alkaline waste that in past geologic ages was part of the bed of an inland sea. Emigrants heading west crossed a desolate expanse to the Truckee River; those traveling south came to the lower Carson. *(Continued on page 120)*

Leaden and sluggish, the Humboldt River winds toward its sink in the Nevada desert. Travelers on the California Trail had little choice but to follow the Humboldt's meandering, 390-mile course; it provided the only water and grass. But the emigrants came to hate the river's monotony, the heat and dust, the drudgery of repeated crossings, and the water's increasingly salty taste.

JOHN AGNONE, N.G.S. STAFF

"I wanted to prove it to myself"

Barbara Maat trudges a continental path to confirm that it can be done. "I was fascinated and awed by the pioneers' walking across the country. I could hardly believe it." So the mother of two from East Bridgewater, Massachusetts, set off herself, taking six months, $1,300, and a lot of pluck to complete the hike from Independence, Missouri, to Sacramento, California. Below, she follows the route of the California Trail along Interstate 80 east of Reno, Nevada. At left, she awakens near Donner Pass in the Sierra Nevada; at right, she breakfasts on banana flakes and sunflower seeds. When her feet hurt badly after 360 miles, she accepted a kindly farmer's gift of a golf cart for her backpack.

Tragedy of the Donner Party

Battling deep snow, members of the ill-fated Donner party of 1846-47 struggle toward a pass in the Sierra Nevada in a desperate effort to escape winter's entrapment. Dissension and fatigue forced them to turn back to their camp and a nightmare that ended in robbery, murder, starvation, and cannibalism.

OPPOSITE: PAINTING BY WILLIAM GILBERT GAUL, 1891, COURTESY THE OAKLAND MUSEUM HISTORY DEPARTMENT; ABOVE: CALIFORNIA DEPARTMENT OF PARKS AND RECREATION; RIGHT AND FOLLOWING PAGES: DAVID HISER

Of the 87 who took a new route angling south of the Great Salt Lake, five died in the desert and 35 in the Sierra snows; only 47 finally arrived at Sutter's Fort in California. James F. Reed and his wife, Margaret, above, and all four Reed children survived. Before reaching the Sierra, the group had banished Reed for killing another emigrant during a dispute. Reed made his way to Sutter's Fort, and led two of seven attempts to rescue the snowbound party. A tiny doll, shown nearly actual size, solaced eight-year-old Patty Reed during her November-to-March ordeal. FOLLOWING PAGES: *Skiers trail through virgin snow in today's mist-shrouded Donner Pass.*

117

For the wagon trains, the two crossings were almost equally bad. The deep sand, choking dust, and cruel heat took their toll on humans and animals alike. For two to four days of travel, there was no drinkable water except at mineral-filled Boiling Springs.

James Avery Pritchard, a gold-rush emigrant, described his trepidation: ". . . we intended to commence the much dreaded journey across the 45 mile dessert of Salt, fire, and I had like to have said Brimstone." Sarah Royce wrote, "For a long time not a word was spoken save occasionally to the cattle . . . [whose] heads drooped as they pressed their shoulders . . . wearily against the bows."

Yet all but a few emigrants made it to water and grass, though many lost their animals and their belongings. At the Truckee River, diarist John Steele told of the "luxury once more to recline beneath the shadow of a tree." Of the people who straggled to safety at the river, he said, "Ragged, dusty, weary and starved they come . . . with bruised, blistered, and bleeding feet, plodding through the hot sand. . . ."

To me it seemed incomprehensible that they made it at all. Through the autumn, I explored the Forty-Mile Desert several times by four-wheel-drive vehicle, on horseback with a latter-day wagon train, and on foot. I followed the way of the emigrants, to this day marked by bits of the once profuse debris of rusted barrel hoops, remnants of wagons, pottery shards, fragments of sun-purpled glass, and bleached bones of oxen and mules.

The sounds of creaking wagons pulled by straining oxen and mules came eerily to life when I joined the wagon train for its reenacted journey into the Forty-Mile Desert. Reining my horse away from the caravan, I rode to the top of a sand ridge and followed it along. Below me, the path of the wagons could be traced for miles by the haze of dust churned up by their iron-rimmed wheels. The sounds of cracking whips, shouted muleskinner oaths when mules tangled their traces, clinking of harness chains, and rumbling of wheels were carried up to me by the desert wind. I was fascinated by the slower but sure progress of one wagon pulled by three spans of black oxen, bringing to mind the old pioneer argument about which were better as wagon teams, mules or oxen.

I rode down off the ridge and fell in beside stocky Hap Magee, a rancher whose hobby is training oxen for western parades. In between his shouts of "Gee!" and "Haw!" he said, "Give me oxen every time. Even these young steers just getting broke to the yoke are steady as a rock."

From Ragtown, where pioneers paused to wash their tattered rags of clothing, the emigrant trail generally followed the Carson River westerly into the Sierra Nevada. Now paralleled by modern highways for many miles, the route is easily distinguishable by ruts cut deeply into the soil and the piles of cast-aside rock that flank them.

In autumn the tree-lined Carson River is placid and cool after the heat of the naked desert. Its winding course is marked by giant cottonwoods, through whose leafy canopy filters golden sunlight.

Seemingly endless tracks reach to the horizon in Nevada's Forty-Mile Desert, west of the sinks where the Humboldt and Carson rivers end. The traces possibly record the route of emigrant wagons. In this alkali country, salt crystals concentrate in depressions after rainstorms, so such tracks remain barren through the years.

DAVID HISER

One branch of the trail goes past Fort Churchill, an adobe ruin overlooking the river. Most of the wood from abandoned Churchill went to build nearby Buckland Station, an important stopover and trading post on the California Trail after 1870. Samuel Buckland was known as an honest trader—a rare reputation in pioneer days.

Provisionless travelers could not hope for mercy from the unscrupulous traders who came back over the Sierra from California. In 1850 John Steele wrote, "Near our camp are several trading posts where, had we money, we might purchase flour and bacon at three dollars a pound. . . . Many a fine outfit has been sold by hungry men for a few pounds of flour and bacon." Steele related how some transients offered to sell a mule for 25 pounds of flour. The trader offered six, and the men replied, "We'll eat the mule first." And they did.

On an Indian-summer day, I traced one of the main gold-rush routes, paralleling the Carson River at the foot of the Sierra, then following the river's boulder-strewn West Fork to the precipitous climb up to Kit Carson Pass. I began south of Carson City in the river valley's lush setting of farmland and gracious century-old homes.

In emigrant times, Carson Valley was a respite of clear water and wild grass that must have lulled senses from the realities of the task ahead. Where the valley narrows and pinches out in the Sierra foothills, it became another matter indeed. At first glance, the abrupt thrusting-up of the mountain barrier seemed impassable. Then, gradually, a cleft appeared, a rock-clogged canyon cut through the mountains by the brawling, icy West Fork.

James Pritchard waxed poetic as he climbed through the cleft to higher ground. He described the country as "certainly one of the grandest and most sublimely picturesque Scenories that I ever beheld . . . [mountains] reareing their lofty summits to an elevation that seemed to stagger human calculation . . . Pine trees . . . 7 & 8 feet in diameter and 200 feet in length." As his party toiled up the mountain above Red Lake, 14 mules hitched to each wagon in turn and all the men pushing and chocking the wheels, he told of the awesome chasms beneath them. One abandoned pair of wagon wheels that they shoved off the trail "bounded with such force that it touched nothing for several hundred yards and in its erial flight it cleared the tops of some of the tallest Pine trees."

At the top came Kit Carson Pass, but that crossed only the first ridgeline of the range. Emigrant Pass, over the second ridge, reached 9,600 feet, the highest point on any wagon trail across the Sierra; from there it was downhill to the goldfields.

The trail went by Tragedy Springs, where three forward scouts of a group of veterans of the Mormon Battalion were killed, apparently by Indians, in 1848. The Carson wagon route over the Sierra was cut, west to east, by 45 former members of the same Mormon unit that the year before had broken a wagon trail across the Southwest. Now they were headed at last for Salt Lake City.

Off a little side road near cliffbound Silver Lake, I found the springs and a grave, a silent spot in the deep forest gloom. A marker describes how members of the group noticed arrows and a newly made mound. When they opened it, they found the burned, arrow-pierced bodies of their three missing friends.

But as grimly dramatic as the incident was, it pales beside the mass tragedy of the Donner party in the winter of 1846-47 on the more northerly Truckee River route high in the central Sierra.

Except for the horrific circumstances surrounding that expedition, Donner Pass might well have been named after one of the three men who earlier engineered the first successful wagon-train assault to go all the way across the mountains. The three were onetime trapper Elisha Stevens, Missouri farmer Martin Murphy, and a physician named John Townsend.

The Stevens-Murphy-Townsend party set out from Missouri in March 1844, two years before the Donner expedition. It comprised 23 men, 8 women, and 15 children, all of whom managed to survive straits almost identical to those of the Donner party.

As far as the Rockies, the group had the guidance of an old mountain man, Caleb Greenwood. But Greenwood had traveled only a pack trail across the Sierra Nevada; and beyond Fort Hall, Idaho, he and the party simply followed wagon tracks of mountain man Joe Walker, who had broken trail the year before. They fared reasonably well down some 360 miles of the Humboldt River lifeline. When they reached the Forty-Mile Desert they met an Indian named Truckee, who guided them west, instead of south on Walker's path, to a grass-lined river with headwaters high in the Sierra.

In appreciation, the pioneers named the river Truckee. Working their way upstream to what they called Truckee Meadows, the present site of Reno, they proceeded into the mountains. High canyon walls forced as many as ten river crossings to advance a single mile. Soon heavy snow buried the grass, but the oxen were saved when they came upon patches of tall reeds. Where the Truckee forked with a creek, the party split forces. The main group followed the creek (now called Donner) looking for a direct pass over the mountains. On horseback the smaller unit, including two women, became the first whites known to have visited Lake Tahoe.

The main party left six wagons under guard and continued with five. Climbing a thousand-foot granite slope—this included hauling the wagons by chains and windlass up a ten-foot vertical wall—they advanced ten miles and conquered what is now Donner Pass. Ten miles or so beyond, a snowstorm broke upon them. Martin Murphy's wife gave birth to a child. The men decided to build a cabin and leave the women, children, and most of the food before pushing on to Sutter's Fort 85 miles away.

After incredibly frustrating delays, including impressment into Army service to fight the Mexicans, the men returned three months later to collect those left behind. Although a few women and children had to resort to eating hides before the rescue, everyone lived, including the newborn baby.

The contrast between the ending of this group's story and that of the later Donner party is startling. Part of (Continued on page 128)

Morning chore becomes a magic moment on the trail near Fallon, Nevada, beside the Carson River. A cowboy takes horses to water during a reenactment of emigrant-trail days. Pioneers used horses for scouting and livestock wrangling, though most chose oxen or mules to pull their wagons. This oasis marked the end of the southbound trail across the Forty-Mile Desert.

DAVID HISER

Sierra Nevada: the Carson River route

*Under luminous skies, a gnarled old juniper and sun-dappled aspens grace
the Carson River route through the Sierra Nevada. Aspens frame jewel-like Caples
Lake, the pine forest on its far shore, and the last snow-patched summits of the
Sierra's western ridgeline. Beyond lies the Sacramento Valley at the end of the trail.
Junipers, with their wind-twisted forms (right) and intricate pattern of needles
(detail at left, below), help clothe the Carson River canyon with a mantle of
greenery. At Carson Pass, in the eastern ridge, Kit Carson carved his name on a
tree in 1844; today visitors can see a section of the trunk on display at Sutter's Fort.*

CAROL A. ENQUIST, N.G.S. STAFF

DAVID HISER (ABOVE, RIGHT, AND OPPOSITE)

St. Joe to Sacramento: the Pony Express

Without wasting a second, a Pony Express rider leaves his tired horse at a relay station and bolts off on a fresh one. Nearly 200 stations dotted the route between St. Joseph, Missouri, and Sacramento, California. The 1,966-mile gallop took 8 to 15 days, depending on the weather. Financially

ABOVE: "COMING AND GOING OF THE PONY EXPRESS" BY FREDERIC REMINGTON, 1900; COURTESY THE THOMAS GILCREASE INSTITUTE OF AMERICAN HISTORY AND ART, TULSA, OKLAHOMA

a failure during its brief operation—from April 1860 until the completion of the ocean-to-ocean telegraph in October 1861—the Pony Express nevertheless counts as a remarkable achievement in the history of communications. Letters from the Atlantic Coast went by regular mail to St. Joseph, then by Pony Express to the Pacific Coast. The initial rate, $5 for each half-ounce plus U.S. postage, later dropped to $1. The company purchased only the best horses, and advertised for "young, skinny, wiry fellows, not over 18. Must be expert riders, willing to risk death daily. Orphans preferred. . . ." The service completed 308 runs in each direction with the loss of only one rider, killed by Indians. Billy Cody (far left), famous later as Buffalo Bill, became an express rider at 14. Richard Erastus Egan (top of page) once rode 330 miles—his own run plus that of a friend who wanted to visit his sweetheart. Egan, a Mormon, became a bishop. Other Mormon riders included Billy and John Fisher and Johnny Hancock (left to right).

the explanation is found in the more extreme weather the Donner party encountered, and its fewer provisions after following a more grueling route; but much of it lies in the unpredictability of each individual's reactions and judgment when confronted by catastrophe.

Oregon-bound J. M. Shively did not equivocate about the human condition of those caught up in the westering process: Emigrants "will quarrel . . . till the company will divide and subdivide . . . let no man leave dependent on his best friend for any thing; for if you do, you will certainly have a blow-out before you get far." His warning could have served as prophecy for the Donner party.

The group was typical in most ways of wagon trains that headed west before the gold rush. It was composed of family units: the Donners, Reeds, Breens, Eddys, Murphys, Wolfingers, Kesebergs, and their hired hands, plus a few lone men such as C. T. Stanton. Most of the husbands were rather well-off farmers or merchants.

In addition to a family history of pioneering by some like the Donners, inspiration for the long journey to California lay in a book called *The Emigrants' Guide to Oregon and California*. Written by Lansford W. Hastings, a young Ohio lawyer who had visited the Pacific Coast, the book caused a sensation east of the Missouri River. Hastings painted glowing visions of a California of the future, and the prospects of land, health, and wealth were so intoxicating that no one bothered to question his sincerity. Actually, Hastings was an unprincipled promoter and opportunist.

As members of a huge company of emigrants, the Donner party in 1846 traveled the main Oregon Trail across the Great Plains with comparative ease. Their misfortunes began when they separated from the main group at the Little Sandy River 20 miles west of South Pass, to take the Hastings route by way of Fort Bridger. This, claimed Hastings—who had just departed with another train— would reduce the distance to California by 300 to 400 miles.

Mountain man Jim Bridger had a trading post at Fort Bridger. Virginia Reed, one of the survivors of the tragedy, wrote in later life that Bridger and his partner Vasques "being employed by Hastings . . . sounded the praises" of the new road, and that the two men assured the emigrants that a 45-mile desert south of the Great Salt Lake was "the only bad part." The Donners could not know that Hastings and Bridger had never tried out the shortcut with wagons.

Numbering at this point 74 men, women, and children in 20 wagons, the party dutifully followed the week-old tracks of Hastings himself and two lead groups. Hastings, however, was lost much of the time, so the trail he left was long and circuitous. When the Donner group reached the Wasatch Range, Virginia Reed recalled years later, "There was absolutely no road, not even a trail." The ax-wielding men used up energy, tempers, and 15 days cutting through 36 miles of heavily wooded terrain. When the party, now with 13 newcomers, had done so, it was only to find in northwestern Utah a hundred miles of dry valleys, mountains, and glittering salt desert. They barely made it across in nine days and several nights of arduous travel. Left behind were numerous wagons and lost cattle. Exhausted and frightened, they cursed Hastings and his lies. For two weeks more, his tracks led them the long way to a point on the Humboldt River still two weeks from the Forty-Mile Desert.

Disaster began to follow disaster. When the handsome, popular John Snyder beat his oxen with the butt end of a whip, James Reed attempted to stop him. The younger man turned his fury and his whip on Reed and Mrs. Reed, and Reed killed him with a knife. For his act, some men of the party almost hanged Reed, but finally decided instead to banish him into the desert without provisions or arms. It was a sentence of death. But in the night Virginia Reed, then only 12 years old, and a hired man crept out to give her father food and weapons to help him survive.

All along the Humboldt River, aggressive Paiute Indians stole cattle and horses or wounded the animals with arrows. By the time the party reached the Forty-Mile Desert, the train had been reduced to 15 wagons and carried very little food.

From then on, it was every family for itself. The Reeds and Eddys had lost all their cattle to the Indians. They left their goods and walked the dreaded desert, adults carrying small children. When the Breens refused to give a drink of water to Eddy's thirsty child, Eddy took it at gunpoint. One wagon owner had already pushed out an old man, leaving him to walk—and die.

When the group reached Truckee Meadows, there began a brief time of hope. Bachelor C. T. Stanton, who had been sent ahead to Sutter's Fort, returned with seven mules loaded with provisions, and two of Sutter's Indian cowboys. He also brought word that James Reed had made it through to California alive, and was trying to organize a relief expedition.

By now it was late October, and snow on the Sierra was portending an early winter. But the oxen were exhausted, and the Donner party let them eat and rest five days at Truckee Meadows. Then, fording the icy stream repeatedly, the group climbed more than 50 miles to the granite-walled pass destined to take the Donner name. Deep snow stopped them. Near the lake below the pass the 81 people, half of them children, took shelter in hastily thrown-up cabins and tents, even lean-tos and a brush wigwam. Snowed in, huddling in bitter cold, they waited for the storm's end.

It never really came. Six times, groups tried to escape. Only part of one group succeeded in reaching, more dead than alive, a rancher's house after a month of extreme suffering.

In the camp below the pass, Patrick Breen kept a diary—the only on-the-scene record of the tragedy that followed. It tells a story of mounting horror among the 66 left there. On November 20, 1846, he wrote, "We now have killed most part of our cattle. . . ." From then on, he recorded the storms and the rising snowpack from "about three feet" to five feet—"no liveing thing without wings can get about"—and finally 13 feet. On Christmas Day he wrote, ". . . offered our prayers to God this Cherimass morning the prospect is apalling but hope in God *Amen*." *(Continued on page 136)*

ABOVE: MELINDA BERGE; BELOW: DAVID HISER

Oasis at Black Rock

Vapor rises from hot Black Rock Spring, an oasis at the foot of the Black Rock Range in Nevada's northwestern desert. Out of empty flatlands to the west rise the sawtooth Calico Mountains. Thirsty, weary emigrants bound for California walked through this desolate country to avoid the more southerly Forty-Mile Desert and the high Sierra passes; ironically, for most the route brought even greater difficulties. At left, Tom Hunt and Bob Griffin (wearing hat) repair a marker beside the trail.

Sunset in the promised land: Evening's glow bathes rolling foothills in the California

gold country, gilding a wandering stream where prospectors once sought bonanzas.

Fighting, racing, restraining a drunken youth; reading from the Bible or doing

household chores: Gold miners spend a Sunday away from the rigors of the workweek.

It was February 18 before the first of a series of rescue parties arrived. The final and total disintegration of the Donner group, with each individual struggling to stay alive, is portrayed in simple sentences whose impact is chilling:

"Mrs Murphy said here yesterday that thought she would Commence on Milt. & eat him. The Donnos [Donners] . . . told . . . folks that they commence to eat the dead people 4 days ago. . . ."

And on March 1, 1847, Breen's final entry:

"there has 10 men arrived this morning from bear valley with provisions we are to start in two or three days"

It was to be seven more weeks before it was all over. Of the 87 who cut through the Wasatch, only 47 survived the entire trip.

Words of 12-year-old Virginia Reed serve as epitaph to the fate of the Donner party. They were contained in a letter to her cousin, written soon after she and her mother were reunited with her father in California: "never take no cutofs and hury along as fast as you can."

I arrived at Alder Creek near Donner Lake on October 28, almost 132 years after George and Jacob Donner and their families were snowbound there in 1846. I was with ramrod-straight Everett Harris, a retired engineering professor who has been marking and writing about emigrant trails for 45 of his 75 years. He had traced the

California Trail for me from bustling Reno up the Truckee River as it wound through the rugged backcountry of the lower Sierra.

At Alder Creek, Dr. Harris led me to a tall, venerable pine tree. "Our best calculation is that George Donner set up a tent-and-pine-branch hovel for his family here, and his brother Jacob built another in that grove of tamarack trees over there. Both of them died in their hovels," he said.

On that late autumn day when grass-lined Alder Creek was serene and golden, it was hard to imagine the suffering and brutalization that had occurred here. But at Donner Lake, a cold wind sprang up as we viewed the site where most of the party had been snowbound, and I knew a sense of foreboding. It was here that Brig. Gen. Stephen W. Kearny in the spring of 1847, only weeks after the last of the group was rescued, had come upon the tragic spectacle of dismembered bodies and stripped bones.

I came back to Donner Lake again soon after. This time, I was to observe in small part what the members of the Donner party must have encountered. The sun-kissed autumn days were gone. Winter's first storm had tumbled over the mountain, the trees were tossed by a howling wind, and the pass above was obscured by falling snow.

On a road near Alder Creek, I found the person I was searching out. She was Barbara Maat, a young woman who had started months before to repeat the trek of the Donner party from Missouri to Sutter's Fort. She had walked nearly 2,000 miles along the Donners' route. The snowstorm had caught her the night before.

"I cried when I woke up to see the snow," she said. "I was overwhelmed when I imagined their misery and terror."

A short time later I watched her diminutive figure stride off into the storm, and I knew that the determination that had motivated the pioneers was not altogether gone.

After the Donner tragedy, until the madness of the gold rush, the Truckee River and Donner Pass were avoided by emigrants. In 1848 about 25 families went up the Carson River and over Carson Pass after meeting the Mormon Battalion veterans who had just opened the trail. Ten other wagons followed Peter Lassen on his Applegate "shortcut" from the Humboldt across northwestern Nevada.

As with the Hastings cutoff, the Applegate-Lassen route had worse deserts than the Forty-Mile Desert, and was no shortcut at all. It was, in fact, longer to Sutter's Fort by 200 miles. Author-historian Sessions Wheeler points out that the original Applegate road was intended as another way to Oregon. To lure the emigrants to his ranch, aspiring empire builder Lassen told them his route would outflank the Sierra, then turn back south. Lost for two months, he and the party were saved by Oregonians on their way to the new goldfields.

Lassen sent a false account to eastern newspapers; and in 1849 emigrant leaders saw his ruts turning off the Humboldt and followed. By the time they realized how vast the wastelands were, hundreds of wagons were blindly following them. Back at the Humboldt turnoff, rumor solidified into a sign: "Only 110 miles to the diggings."

About 8,000, or more than a third of that year's stream of

Traveling drugstore visits a mining camp in the Sierra foothills. Several men interrupt their gold-panning to help an ailing fellow worker. Many doctors who marched west with the gold rush soon became too busy caring for the sick and injured to look for gold themselves. Others such as Dr. Justin Gates, who owned a drugstore in Sacramento and the wagon pictured here, made profit enough from business to see no lure in mining.

emigrants, took the "shortcut." They lived to regret it—if, indeed, they survived at all. Many lost everything, dropping their belongings along the roadside, which became one long junkpile. October snow overtook them in the Sierra, and a massive Donner-like tragedy would have been almost inevitable had not the territorial governor of California, Brig. Gen. Persifor F. Smith, anticipated disaster and sent out military relief parties.

One of the many diarists on the Lassen trail was Alonzo Delano of Illinois, who later became a California author of note. Delano railed against "false reports and misrepresentation . . . . instead of getting rid of a forty-five-mile sand plain [the Forty-Mile Desert], we had actually crossed the [naked] desert where it was a hundred miles broad." Delano also told of "the howling of hungry wolves," and constant Indian stealing of cattle and horses or disabling of the stock with stone-tipped arrows.

Then came that meticulous and voluminous chronicler, J. Goldsborough Bruff, a District of Columbia cartographer and former West Pointer. His company of 66 men and 17 mule-drawn wagons was organized along military lines. From the turnoff to Black Rock Spring, some 50 miles, he recorded 511 dead oxen.

The Black Rock Desert lies to the northeast of Pyramid Lake in northwestern Nevada. It is as barren as a moonscape, an almost perfectly level expanse of crusted white, somewhat salty clay silt. On its surface heat waves create mirages of lakes, trees, and greenery. Despite these illusions, there is scarcely a blade of grass to break the starkness. The whole area is part of the ancient Lahontan Lake bed, which also includes the Humboldt and Carson sinks.

For the pioneers, what a forbidding obstacle! Yet to travel across the Black Rock Desert today by four-wheel-drive vehicle can be an exhilarating experience. Photographers David Hiser and Melinda Berge and I were in one vehicle, and our guides, Thomas Hunt and Robert S. Griffin, were in another. We skimmed across the expanse as free as the wind, sending up white plumes of pulverized silt.

Hunt, an artist and author from Palo Alto, recalled that one chronicler "wrote that he could have jumped from carcass to carcass of dead oxen and mules along this trail all the way across the desert."

Black Rock is a 400-foot-tall conical mass that Dr. Vincent Gianella, dean of Nevada geologists, discovered is not a volcano, as once thought, nor lava flows like its namesake range, but marine sediment of volcanic debris. Approaching its base, we slowed down and drove cautiously. Here bogs created by floodwaters of spring are all but undetectable on the flatness, and can easily trap the unwary. In fact, two deer hunters who started across the desert shortly after we did sank into a bog in their pickup truck. Their calls for help on citizens-band radio finally brought rescue after three days.

We stopped at the grassy border of Black Rock Spring, a slightly saline pool that sometimes bubbles when gases come up with the hot spring water. Griffin, a Frémont scholar, said he had measured its temperature at levels as high as 140 degrees.

From the spring we drove north following old wagon ruts into

Two words turn gloom to glee on the arrival of a young woman at a mining camp. In the goldfields of the early 1850's, men greatly outnumbered women: The town of Rich Bar, California, had a population of 2,500 men and four women. Another early engraving shows a banner hanging from the eaves of a house: "Lucky Miners House But No Wife."

MARRIED MUM ?   NO SIR!

sagebrush desert along the western flank of the Black Rock Range. At Double Hot Springs I was warned of the danger of slipping down its steep banks into the water. Bob Griffin said he had taken readings here above 200 degrees—with the mineral water actually boiling at the 4,000-foot elevation. When emigrants' oxen stumbled into these pools, they were well cooked before they could be pulled out.

We wound our way along the tortuous desert trail at two miles an hour, the powdered dust rising around us so thick that we repeatedly stopped until it had cleared enough for us to go on. Where the emigrants turned north into High Rock Canyon, we made camp. The sun went down, and we felt the icy chill of the desert night and an errant wind. Our campfire of sagebrush was a lonely pinpoint of light in the vastness of mountain and desert.

As we ate our supper of steak and beans, Hunt and Griffin told of their efforts to preserve portions of the Black Rock Desert, the many-hued Calico Mountains bounding it on the west, and High Rock Canyon—which we were yet to see—as the Emigrant Trail National Monument. "There are some 750,000 acres involved, most of it held by the Bureau of Land Management," Tom Hunt explained. "Except for a ranch or two, the land is unpopulated. What better place to preserve an unspoiled region that played such an important part in our national heritage?" (A short time later I learned that a significant portion of the area, about one-seventh, had been entered in the National Register of Historic Places as the Applegate-Lassen Trail.)

Reluctant to take off anything except my boots, I rolled into my

Gold! The search goes on

Tom Belichick (below, left) and Rick Franz work an old mine they and four partners have leased in California. They drill and dynamite in the evening, and in the morning muck out the gravel and clear the bedrock. "Then we scrape away everything from the face and hunt and pick around with knives, looking for that glory hole." At right, Don (Stoney) Albrecht demonstrates old-fashioned sluicing. He shovels gold-bearing sand into a sluice box in the water; the creek will wash away the sand and leave the heavier gold behind. (For his own mining, Albrecht

builds dredging machines.) In the foreground: some of the gold collected over ten years from these same waters. At lower right, nuggets form a natural necklace in black sand at the bottom of a pan.

ALL BY DAVID HISER

frigid sleeping bag that night only to be awakened by the "howling of hungry wolves" that Alonzo Delano had written about. Actually, this time they were coyotes that had come down to ring our campsite.

We awoke at daybreak to watch the changing colors on the rim-rocks above. When the sun rose, it revealed a sky of purest blue dye, so free of pollution it seemed unreal. Setting out again, we penetrated High Rock Canyon, a knifelike passage between 200-foot reddish cliffs that in places appear almost to come together at their summits. Here we found deep caves where Indians had lived and where gold-rush transients and others had chiseled their names or painted them in axle grease. It was here, also, that they rested before continuing the last hundreds of deadly miles to the gold country of California.

In January of 1848 hired man James W. Marshall found gold in the tailrace of John Sutter's sawmill on the South Fork of the American River. By 1849 the rush to California was on, and with it the complexion of western emigration changed. Family groups and neighbors westering together gave way to a glut of fortune seekers, almost all men, from every part of the United States and foreign lands as well. Historian Dale Morgan described it: "A more profound national experience than the Gold Rush, intimately invading as it did the life and society of every State . . . would be difficult to name."

In 1849 alone, an estimated 22,500 travelers crowded the California Trail in a stream of wagons, handcarts, men on mules and horses, men on foot. They were from all walks of life, scholars and professional men as well as vagabonds and jailbirds. Within a year after emigrant E. Gould Buffum arrived in 1848 and called it "an untenanted plain," Sacramento was transformed into a city of 12,000.

It was only the beginning. In the years ahead, towns and mining camps sprang up almost overnight along the length of the western Sierra slope. Every potential gold-bearing stream was thronged with miners and the merchants who fed and equipped them. Some would find fortune and manage to keep it, others would squander it, and many would return penniless to distant homes. But most would decide to follow other occupations and settle down in a California that only in 1846 had become part of the United States.

Coloma, on the site of that first fateful gold strike of 1848, is today a sleepy little community in a soft setting of grassy, rolling hills studded with scrub oaks. It exists mainly as a living museum of gold-rush days, drawing curious tourists from all parts of the world.

Wandering up the quiet main street, I found young blacksmith Charles Butterfield working at his forge in a soot-blackened old shop. We talked about some unsung heroes of the emigrant trails: the pioneer smiths who, in his words, "jury-rigged" wheels and iron rims all the long way across the unpeopled continent.

"When you consider what they went through," the blacksmith said, "you come to understand they must have wanted to get to California awful bad."

It was as good a pronouncement as I was likely to hear of the epic that was the California Trail.

"If you don't know the technique of panning, you lose more gold than you find. I don't lose any," says Irby E. (Blackrock) Hosea of Meadow Vista, California. Blackrock has been prospecting for gold for 48 of his 76 years. "The older I get, the colder the river water seems to get. It's still fun, but it's hard work, too." DAVID HISER

Pathway in the Desert

By Don Dedera

A grumbling thunderstorm broods round the bald stone brows of Cochise Head. Heat presses down from an arching midday sun. Up the draw a coyote yodels; close by, a round-tailed squirrel barks an alarm from the arms of a mesquite tree. Off ridges darkly dotted with thrifty conifers and shrubs wafts a perfume pungent with turpentine and musk.

At the trailhead I leave my car and start to walk. Apache Pass! Each turn in the path conjures shades of ancient mastodon hunters, of sophisticated potters, of intrepid explorers, of dusty columns of dragoons, of prospectors and furtive outlaws, of staunch emigrant wagoners, or of painted bands of red warriors. Long ago they all walked or rode through wilderness lands that eventually became the American Southwest. They traveled along, fought over, and found graves beside a trail already thousands of years old.

In time the trail borrowed a name from an Arizona river: the Gila, pronounced *Hee*-lah, a Spanish corruption of an Indian word meaning "salty."

This day, hiking alone, I welcome the company of the Gila Trail's ghosts. For me it is a sentimental journey. As a young newspaperman 20 years ago I visited this area of southeastern Arizona and sadly reported upon a monument to apathy and vandalism. Apache Pass and its abandoned military post were scarred by off-road vehicles, picked bare by scavengers, peppered by riflemen. My published lament was only one of many efforts that ultimately led to the establishment of Fort Bowie as a protected national historic site.

The path descends sandy gullies and climbs thorn-strewn slopes, past foundation stones of the old Butterfield Stage station, past a disheveled cemetery, past a replica of an Apache camp. Even the surface of the ground suggests a mosaic of conflict: In the rough gravel it is easy to imagine glass splinters and pottery shards, flakes of arrowheads, spent bullets, bits of pioneer metal junk—reminders of a time when cultures here were in bloody collision. Much has changed in a century of peace, but much remains the same as on the day the great Apache leader Cochise spoke these words:

The Gila Trail

Westerly routes from Santa Fe and El Paso joined in Apache country to form the Gila Trail. Traversing the deserts of the southwestern frontier, it took a course determined by sources of water and passages through the mountains. Soldiers and emigrants, miners and mail carriers, freighters and outlaws traveled the trail beginning in the 1840's. In time trains, autos, and airplanes followed their lead.

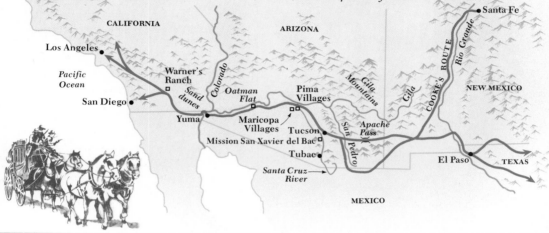

"When I was young I walked all over this country, east and west, and saw no other people than the Apaches. After many summers I walked again and found another race of people had come to take it. How is it? Why is it . . . that the Apaches wait to die. . . ?"

Ahead of me the land grudgingly opens along dry creek beds. Everything is dry. Trees of tiny tentative leaf wave desiccated bean pods. Cured grasses crackle in the slight wind. Wrinkled cactus competes with agave and yucca. Lizards scurry. My thirst intensifies.

LOWELL GEORGIA   KERBY SMITH   LOWELL GEORGIA

Once the remote threshold of a great adventure, now a cosmopolitan crossroads, El Paso reflects the rosy morning light. About 1850 a small American settlement grew up on the north bank of the Rio Grande opposite a thriving Mexican town founded in 1659. Later, emigrants stopped here to stock up on supplies before funneling westward through the adjacent mountain pass to the Gila Trail. Today's El Paso and its twin city, Ciudad Juárez, Mexico, comprise a metropolis of more than a million people.

Presently the path arrives at a shady grotto bearing a ledge brimming with a barrel-size pool of cool water. I drink deeply and gratefully from Apache Spring, as did those who preceded me: Cochise himself, and the indestructible Geronimo. Generals Phil Sheridan and George Crook. Outlaws Curly Bill and Billy the Kid.

Just as this unfailing source of water was crucial to the Indians' possession of their hunting grounds, so Apache Spring likewise assumed strategic importance for "another race of people. . . ." To hold the spring and Apache Pass, Fort Bowie was built in 1862 by Union soldiers of the First California Volunteers.

A few minutes more and I arrive at the adobe ruins of the fort. Atop a towering white flagpole, a Stars and Stripes of heroic size snaps above the parade ground. The only other modern touch is a 10-by-12-foot building that must rank as one of the smallest ranger station-museums in the national park system.

Ranger Bill Hoy is steeped in the lore of Apache Pass and the Gila Trail. He leans back in his chair, locks his hands on his graying hair, and asks a most unusual question:

"When you were walking in, did you feel their presence?"

I stammer, "Well, yes, but frankly I wondered if a grown man should let his imagination carry him away like that."

Bill laughs. "That's exactly the experience we're trying to encourage here. You have to *want* to come to Bowie. You don't just drive up and jump out. You have to work a bit to earn your visit here."

Then Hoy talks about the Gila Trail in general: "The Gila River was its backbone, but less than 200 miles of the river bank was passable for wagons. Travelers coming from Santa Fe or El Paso entered Arizona south of the rugged Mogollon and Gila mountains, then

went west a hundred miles to the Santa Cruz River. Turning northward, they followed it for another hundred miles to its junction with the Gila. Farther west, after the Gila joined the Colorado, the trail pushed on across sand, then over mountains to reach the Pacific."

Archaeologists infer human use of the Gila Trail more than 20,000 years ago from skeletal remains unearthed in 1971 near the California-Mexico border. Evidence abounds that prehistoric peoples traveled the Gila Valley trading in shells, turquoise, and metal.

Probably the first non-Indians to visit this region were Alvar Núñez Cabeza de Vaca and three companions. Shipwrecked on the Texas coast in 1528, they wandered almost to the Gulf of California before stumbling into the Spanish outpost of Culiacán in 1536.

Inspired by stories the four had picked up from Indians, Francisco Vásquez de Coronado set out in 1540 in search of the mythical Seven Golden Cities of Cíbola. The expedition, which included 225 Spaniards on horseback, 60 foot soldiers, nearly a thousand Indians, and large herds of livestock, penetrated the future United States as far as Kansas. The adventurers found no gold, but they acquainted the Indians of the northern frontiers with horses and cattle.

Catholic missionaries followed the explorers. During the 1600's the padres established missions the length of the Rio Grande Valley. Farther west, between 1687 and 1710, the Jesuit priest Eusebio Francisco Kino created out of his enormous energies a parish of 50,000 square miles, reaching from northern Sonora to the Gila River. Kino built 29 missions, baptized thousands of Indians, and pursued at least 50 explorations along the rim of Christendom.

Father Kino was the first to suggest the practicality of overland travel from Tubac to Alta California. Fray Francisco Garcés proved Kino correct when he guided a party of (Continued on page 156)

The Mormon Battalion

Exhausted men of the Mormon Battalion quench their thirst in a California creek and start digging a ramp for the wagon teams. Fifty years later, members of the battalion (right) gather for a portrait in Salt Lake City. In 1846 about 350 Mormons enlisted by the U. S. Army, with their officers and five officers' wives, established a wagon route across the southwestern wilderness from Santa Fe to San Diego. In the scene above, painted by George Martin Ottinger about 1886, the men have just endured three waterless days of walking across deep sand deserts west of the Colorado River. After four months and a thousand miles, the half-starved, ragged soldiers reached the oasis of Warner's Ranch in southern California, then continued on to the Pacific.

Fort at Apache Pass

Wet whisk broom in hand, Fernando Núñez smooths cracks in a protective coating of mud on the ruined adobe walls of Fort Bowie. Established in 1862, the famed Army garrison in the Chiricahua Mountains of southeastern Arizona guarded Apache Pass from Indian attack and secured a vital water supply. At left, George Duran demonstrates a heliograph. Soldiers used these "talking mirrors" to reflect the sun's rays and flash messages in Morse code between 27 relay stations during the last Apache campaigns.

153

"White Dove of the Desert" rises like a sign of peace against a stormy Arizona sky. Founded in 1700 by the Jesuit Eusebio Kino and later completed by the Franciscans, the Mission of San Xavier del Bac near Tucson still functions as a church and school for Papago Indians. The building abounds in rich detail (below): The Franciscan coat-of-arms embellishes the facade; brightly painted plaster cherubs hover throughout the church; a wrought-iron rattlesnake forms the handle of the mesquite door at the main entrance.

soldiers commanded by Lt. Col. Juan Bautista de Anza westward to the Yuma crossing on the Colorado, then across dunes and mountains to the Los Angeles basin in 1774. Two years later Garcés accompanied Anza and 200 men, 45 women, and several babies on the Gila Trail as far as the Colorado. The colonists continued north to found the settlement of Yerba Buena, now San Francisco.

Thus it was that an already historic path—though little used except by Indians—awaited the first recorded Americans to travel along the Gila. With a dozen other beaver trappers, James Ohio Pattie left Santa Fe in 1825, picked up the river's course, and followed it to central Arizona and a point near present-day Phoenix. A few years later with his father, Sylvester, Pattie went all the way to San Diego.

Not far behind were Old Bill Williams, Pauline Weaver, Kit Carson, Baptiste Charbonneau—son of Sacagawea of Lewis and Clark fame—and hundreds of other trappers. These mountain men set a pattern of back-and-forth travel along the Gila Trail.

"It wasn't an hourglass in which all the people like grains of sand trickled in one direction," explains Mrs. Lillian Theobald, Arizona author and retired museum curator. Mrs. Theobald with her late husband, John, prowled the Gila Trail as an avocation. "The trail was a two-way street. Of course, while emigration trails far to the north were rapidly developing in the early 1840's, American use of the southern route was slowed by three formidable obstacles: hostile Indians, Mexican sovereignty, and the desert."

The desert country crossed by the Gila Trail is an overwhelming, enduring reality. If today I am driving to San Diego from San Antonio, there comes a bit west of the 100th meridian a refueling stop called High Lonesome where the road conquers a crest and dives into a distinctly different natural realm.

Behind lie the almost featureless plains of Texas. Ahead unfolds a thousand-mile traverse of rocky hills and harsh valleys, of much heat and little water. I may experience air conditioning, comfortable way stations, and irrigated valleys; but for vast stretches between the infrequent cities, the landscape is shaped by a shortage of rain and an abundance of sunshine.

To those who listen, wrote Joseph Wood Krutch, "the desert speaks . . . with an emphasis quite different from that of . . . the plains. . . . [It] is more likely to provoke awe than to invite conquest."

It took a while for such a sensitive view to evolve. Dr. John S. Griffin, who traveled with Brig. Gen. Stephen Watts Kearny down the Gila in 1846, wrote: ". . . utterly worthless . . . the cactus is the only thing that grows. . . . Every bush in this country is full of thorns . . . every rock you turn over has a tarantula or centipede . . . and . . . the most beautiful specimens of rattlesnakes . . . lizards and scorpions. . . ." A U. S. senator dismissed the region as "just like hell. All it lacks is water and good society."

Of those Americans who presumed to pass over the Gila Trail during the gold rush of 1849-50 and the next three decades, the desert demanded not only physical endurance but also spiritual valor. A

20th-century woman who has traveled the trail scores of times is artist Marjorie Reed Creese, now a resident of Tombstone, Arizona. Inspired by a girlhood friendship with pioneer stage driver Capt. William Banning, she has been setting up her easel to depict episodes and scenes along the Butterfield Overland Mail route, including the portion that followed the Gila Trail, for more than 40 years.

"Few activities are more contemplative than putting paint to canvas," she says. "I've often marveled at the fundamental faith and raw courage required for someone to give up a lush homeland and risk the hardships and dangers along the Gila Trail. Think of the fears a young mother had to stifle in joining her man going west! And the concerns of a head of household must have been almost unbearable."

Yet after 1848—when to end the Mexican War the Republic of Mexico ceded all of Alta California, Nevada, and Utah, most of New Mexico, parts of Colorado and Wyoming, and all of Arizona north of the Gila River—the momentum of migration accelerated. Texas' entry into the Union in 1845 had furthered the dream of the "manifest destiny" of one America spanning the continent. During the summer of 1846, just after Congress declared war, Stephen Kearny led troops of the Army of the West from Fort Leavenworth, Kansas, to New Mexico and took Santa Fe without resistance. To Kearny his orders were quite clear: "Should you conquer and take possession of New Mexico and Upper California . . . you will establish civil governments therein." He promptly selected his best dragoons for a "dash to California." Starting down the Rio Grande Valley, he encountered Kit Carson, Washington-bound with news that the coastal province had fallen to American forces. Sending Carson's message on by courier and impressing the frontiersman as his guide, Kearny and a hundred men mounted on mules swung west to the upper Gila River and the mountains through which it cuts.

The Gila, rising from alpine ponds and snow-fed springs in the highlands of western New Mexico, crosses the full width of Arizona. Before it was dammed extensively in this century, the river could change overnight from a shallow, placid stream to a raging flood.

For five weeks Kearny's troops struggled with the upper Gila's mountains and gorges and the lower river's sandy banks and rocky deserts. Once beyond the Gila's confluence with the Colorado River, they faced barren, burning dunes. The men proved tougher than their mounts; long before the approaches to San Diego, most of the soldiers were afoot. Then, in small but important skirmishes with Mexican forces, they learned that the war wasn't over, after all.

Kearny had begun the journey with wagons, but had sent them back to Santa Fe and instructed Lt. Col. Philip St. George Cooke, assigned to command the Mormon Battalion just arriving from Kansas, to break a wagon trail south of the Gila Mountains.

Cooke's column included about 350 of the volunteers recruited by Brigham Young from the refugees driven out of Nauvoo, Illinois, plus their officers, five officers' wives, and 20 wagons. The battalion followed the Rio Grande, then cut southwest across "a tableland studded with peaks" where no American wheel had ever turned.

"Nothing must stop the United States mail!"

Mail stage thunders into the Butterfield station at Warner's Ranch in a painting by Marjorie Reed Creese. Below, passenger William Hayes Hilton (with beard) climbs above the deepening water in his own 1859 sketch of a Butterfield "mud wagon" fording the Clear Boggy River in present-day Oklahoma. In September 1858 eastbound and westbound stagecoaches of the Butterfield Overland Mail began twice-weekly service between the Mississippi River and California. Ever mindful of John Butterfield's instructions— "Remember, boys, nothing on God's earth must stop the United States mail!"—drivers kept to a demanding timetable, covering 2,800 miles in 25 days. A bugle call from the approaching stage signaled station attendants to harness fresh horses. While they changed teams, the driver delivered and picked up mail, then set off again within minutes. The mail arrived late only three times in three years.

BELOW AND OPPOSITE: COURTESY THE HUNTINGTON LIBRARY, SAN MARINO, CALIFORNIA

PAINTING (1957) FROM "THE COLORFUL BUTTERFIELD OVERLAND STAGE," A COPLEY BOOK

No. 1.] [Sep. 16th, 1858.

OVERLAND MAIL COMPANY.

THROUGH TIME SCHEDULE BETWEEN

ST. LOUIS, MO., MEMPHIS, TENN. } & SAN FRANCISCO, CAL.

GOING WEST.

LEAVE.	DAYS.	Hour.	Distance, Place to Place.	Time allowed.	Av'ge Miles per Hour.
St. Louis, Mo., & Memphis, Tenn. }	Every Monday & Thursday,	8.00 A.M	Miles.	No. Hours	
P. R. R. Terminus, "	" Monday & Thursday,	6.00 P.M	160	10	16
Springfield, "	" Wednesday & Saturday	7.45 A.M	143	$37\frac{3}{4}$	$3\frac{7}{9}$
Fayetteville, "	" Thursday & Sunday,	10.15 A.M	100	$26\frac{1}{2}$	$3\frac{7}{9}$
Fort Smith, Ark.	" Friday & Monday,	3.30 A.M	65	$17\frac{1}{4}$	$3\frac{7}{9}$
Sherman, Texas	" Sunday & Wednesday,	12.30 A.M	205	45	$4\frac{1}{2}$
Fort Belknap. "	" Monday & Thursday,	9.00 A.M	$146\frac{1}{2}$	$32\frac{1}{2}$	$4\frac{1}{2}$
Fort Chadbourn, "	" Tuesday & Friday,	3.15 P.M	136	$30\frac{1}{4}$	$4\frac{1}{2}$
Pecos River, (Em. Crossing.)	" Thursday & Sunday,	3.45 A.M	165	$36\frac{1}{2}$	$4\frac{1}{2}$
El Paso,	" Saturday & Tuesday,	11.00 A.M	$248\frac{1}{2}$	$55\frac{1}{4}$	$4\frac{1}{2}$
Soldier's Farewell	" Sunday & Wednesday,	8.30 P.M	150	$33\frac{1}{2}$	$4\frac{1}{2}$
Tucson, Arizona	" Tuesday & Friday,	1.30 P.M	$184\frac{1}{2}$	41	$4\frac{1}{2}$
Gila River,* "	" Wednesday & Saturday	9.00 P.M	141	$31\frac{1}{2}$	$4\frac{1}{2}$
Fort Yuma, Cal.	" Friday & Monday,	3.00 A.M	135	30	$4\frac{1}{2}$
San Bernardino "	" Saturday & Tuesday,	11.00 P.M	200	44	$4\frac{1}{2}$
Ft. Tejon, (Via Los Angelos.)	" Monday & Thursday,	7.30 A.M	150	$32\frac{1}{2}$	$4\frac{1}{2}$
Visalia, "	" Tuesday & Friday,	11.30 A.M	127	28	$4\frac{1}{2}$
Firebaugh's Ferry, "	" Wednesday & Saturday	5.30 A.M	82	18	$4\frac{1}{2}$
(Arrive) San Francisco,	" Thursday & Sunday,	8.30 A.M	163	27	6

GOING EAST.

LEAVE.	DAYS.	Hour.	Distance, Place to Place.	Time allowed.	Av'ge Miles per Hour.
San Francisco, Cal.	Every Monday & Thursday,	8.00 A.M	Miles.	No. Hours	
Firebaugh's Ferry, "	" Tuesday & Friday,	11.00 A.M	163	27	6
Visalia, "	" Wednesday & Saturday,	5.00 A.M	82	18	$4\frac{1}{2}$
Ft. Tejon, (Via Los Angelos to)	" Thursday & Sunday,	9.00 A.M	127	28	$4\frac{1}{2}$
San Bernardino. "	" Friday & Monday,	5.30 P.M	150	$32\frac{1}{2}$	$4\frac{1}{2}$
Fort Yuma, "	" Sunday & Wednesday,	1.30 P.M	200	44	$4\frac{1}{2}$
Gila River,* Arizona	" Monday & Thursday,	7.30 P.M	135	30	$4\frac{1}{2}$
Tucson, "	" Wednesday & Saturday	3.00 A.M	141	$31\frac{1}{2}$	$4\frac{1}{2}$
Soldier's Farewell,	" Thursday & Sunday,	8.00 P.M	$184\frac{1}{2}$	41	$4\frac{1}{2}$
El Paso, Tex.	" Saturday & Tuesday,	5.30 A.M	150	$33\frac{1}{2}$	$4\frac{1}{2}$
Pecos River, (Em. Crossing.)	" Monday & Thursday	12.45 P.M	$248\frac{1}{2}$	$55\frac{1}{4}$	$4\frac{1}{2}$
Fort Chadbourn, "	" Wednesday & Saturday	1.15 A.M	165	$36\frac{1}{2}$	$4\frac{1}{2}$
Fort Belknap, "	" Thursday & Sunday,	7.30 A.M	136	$30\frac{1}{4}$	$4\frac{1}{2}$
Sherman, "	" Friday & Monday,	4.00 P.M	$146\frac{1}{2}$	$32\frac{1}{2}$	$4\frac{1}{2}$
Fort Smith, Ark.	" Sunday & Wednesday,	1.00 P.M	205	45	$4\frac{1}{2}$
Fayetteville, Mo.	" Monday, & Thursday,	6.15 A.M	65	$17\frac{1}{4}$	$3\frac{7}{9}$
Springfield, "	" Tuesday & Friday,	8.45 A.M	100	$26\frac{1}{2}$	$3\frac{7}{9}$
P. R. R. Terminus, "	" Wednesday & Saturday	10.30 P.M	143	$37\frac{3}{4}$	$3\frac{7}{9}$
(Arrive) St. Louis, Mo., & Memphis, Tenn. }	" Thursday & Sunday,		160	10	16

This Schedule may not be exact—Superintendents, Agents, Station-men, Conductors, Drivers and all employees are particularly directed to use every possible exertion to get the Stages through in quick time, even though they may be ahead of this time.

If they are behind this time, it will be necessary to urge the animals on to the highest speed that they can be driven without injury.

Remember that no allowance is made in the time for ferries, changing teams, &c. It is therefore necessary that each driver increase his speed over the average per hour enough to gain the necessary time for meals, changing teams, crossing ferries, &c.

Every person in the Company's employ will always bear in mind that each minute of time is of importance. If each driver on the route loses fifteen (15) minutes, it would make a total loss of time, on the entire route, of twenty-five (25) hours, or, more than one day. If each one loses ten (10) minutes it would make a total loss of sixteen and one half ($16\frac{1}{2}$) hours, or, the best part of a day.

On the contrary, if each driver gains that amount of time, it leaves a margin of time against accidents and extra delays.

All hands will see the great necessity of promptness and dispatch: every minute of time is valuable as the Company are under heavy forfeit if the mail is behind time.

Conductors must note the hour and date of departure from Stations, the causes of delay, if any, and all particulars. They must also report the same fully to their respective Superintendents.

* The Station referred to on Gila River, is 40 miles west of Maricopa Wells.

JOHN BUTTERFIELD.
Pres't.

*Backpacking Boy
Scouts file along
a desert road on
a bright November
morning. Around
a campfire, members
of another unit—Troop
362 of Glendale,
Arizona—rehash the
day's adventures.
For the ten-mile hike
and an essay on historic
trails, each earns a
special Butterfield
Trail patch.*

A Regular Army officer respected by the Mormons as "strict . . . but impartial . . . brave but austere . . . with a firm manner of speech," Cooke carried his command over a southern spur of the Rockies on curses and curtailed rations. Once beyond that obstacle, he pressed westward from water hole to water hole until he found the San Pedro River. There the Mormons were attacked by longhorn bulls gone feral from ranches abandoned in the wake of Apache raids.

Two days and 65 miles north on the San Pedro, the column turned west and crossed a tableland to the Mexican garrison settlement of Tucson. After camping briefly outside the town—its soldiers and most of its 500 civilians had fled—the battalion walked northwest along the dry bed of the Santa Cruz River to reach the Gila.

Refreshed by the hospitality of the prosperous Pima and Maricopa Indians, the men resumed their march. Rather than trace the great curving course of the Gila through central Arizona, they cut west across 40 waterless miles, forcing the wagons over ridges in an "unremitting struggle with the rude barrenness of a rainless wilderness," wrote Cooke. Intercepting the river again near today's town of Gila Bend, they proceeded west along its channel—despite sand, gullies, and thickets—because of the grass and water it provided.

In early January 1847, the battalion rafted across the Colorado River. Then the "half-starved, worn-out" men had to suffer through the bottomless dunes west of present-day Yuma. Barefoot, "they staggered as they marched," Cooke recorded. Through three hot days and cold nights, men and animals trudged on without a drink.

Even as they anticipated the friendlier ground of California's mountain valleys, new obstacles appeared: high, rugged ridges, and then maddening Box Canyon, one foot too narrow for the wagons. With axes and a single small crowbar the men, led by Cooke himself, hewed a wider passage from solid rock. Ragged and fainting, the Mormons with eight wagons intact finally arrived at Warner's Ranch, a paradise of provisions and warm mineral springs.

"History may be searched in vain for an equal march of infantry," Cooke declared in an order congratulating his men when at last the battalion arrived at San Diego. It had covered two thousand miles from the Missouri River to the Pacific Ocean, a thousand of that in 110 days through arid, primitive wilderness. Only the Battle of the Bulls had tested the Mormons' fighting prowess, but behind them they left a wagon route that, with some variations, would attract cattlemen, emigrants, surveyors, military commanders, prospectors, mail carriers, freighters, and—most important in the shaping of the U. S.-Mexican border—the builders of a transcontinental railroad. Yet, failing to anticipate these American interests, the 1848 treaty that ended the Mexican War proclaimed the Gila River the international boundary.

But reports and maps of Kearny's and Cooke's expeditions publicized the southern route. On the heels of the Mormons, T. J. Trimmer drove 500 longhorns from eastern Texas to California through Mexican territory. Soon the Gila Trail became a river of livestock flowing toward high prices in the new goldfields of California.

The Oatman massacre and the Bascom affair

Survivor of an Indian massacre in 1851 and five years' captivity, Olive Oatman, her chin marked by tattoos, stands for a portrait nearly ten years later. When the Oatman family attempted to cross the Arizona desert alone, Yavapais killed the parents and four children and seized two young girls (a boy escaped). One of the captives died, but Olive lived as a slave until 1856, when an Indian traded her to a white man for horses, food, and blankets. Accounts of Olive's ordeal swept across the country. Above, an 1856 painting by Charles Christian Nahl dramatizes the assault and brutal struggle. Hostile Indians presented a recurring danger along the Gila Trail until the 1880's, although some tribes—Pimas, Papagos, Maricopas, and Yumas—often sold food to pioneers, offered shelter, or acted as guides. At times, even the warlike Apaches tried to live in peace with the ever-encroaching white men. But in 1861 a young and inexperienced Army officer, 2nd Lt. George N. Bascom (left), attempted to arrest the Apache leader Cochise on a charge of kidnaping a rancher's stepson. The incident touched off a dozen years of violent conflict that cost innumerable lives.

Many a gold-feverish forty-niner, too, headed for the Gila Trail by way of the Santa Fe Trail, or across Texas from the Arkansas River, or from San Antonio through El Paso and its low gap in the mountains. Given the alternatives—Great Basin deserts and snowy peaks, or the sea route around Cape Horn, or a tropical traverse of Central America—the Gila Trail seemed a reasonable choice.

Nevertheless, the hazards as well as the hardships were great, and dozens of travelers perished of heat or thirst or were killed by Indians. In 1851 the Royce Oatman family left the protection of a wagon train at Tucson—the Indians seldom attacked large companies—and broached the desert flatlands. West of Gila Bend a band of Yavapais fell upon them, killing the parents and four of the seven children. A boy escaped; of the two captured girls, one survived and was eventually rescued. Published accounts of the tortures inflicted on the Oatman girls were widely read later by California-bound Americans. But they came on anyway.

By 1852 ferries on the Colorado at Yuma had transported across the river an estimated 60,000 emigrants, at first on reed rafts pulled by swimming Indians, later on barges attached to pulley ropes.

In 1853 James Gadsden, American minister to Mexico, negotiated for the United States the purchase of a strip of land south of the Gila encompassing a proposed railroad route to the Pacific as well as the trail already used by thousands of gold seekers. Of the nearly 30,000-square-mile area, Kit Carson grumped, "A wolf could not make a living on it." But many an adventurous American was willing to try. One was Charles D. Poston, a Kentucky lawyer who in 1856 revived the Spanish compound of Tubac, discovered a vein of silver nearby, and thereafter ran a fiefdom financed with the rich ore.

In 1861, when the departure of Union troops left Tubac defenseless against the Apaches, the historic town again was abandoned. Poston, long called the "father of Arizona" for his work to separate it from the Territory of New Mexico, died in squalor. But at his zenith he was elected territorial delegate to Congress, ordered a massive silver inkstand from Tiffany's, consulted with President Lincoln, and dined in London with Mark Twain.

Green winter wheat grows beside newly tilled cotton fields below the rumpled ridges of the Muggins Range near Yuma. Ancestors of the Pima Indians farmed the Arizona desert more than 2,000 years ago, digging nearly 300 miles of irrigation ditches to carry water from the Gila and Salt rivers. Today, these valleys produce some of the highest crop yields in the United States. Canals from the Colorado River irrigate the fields pictured; the Gila—its water impounded by dams farther east—forms for the last 150 miles a dry riverbed except in years of unusually heavy rainfall.

LOWELL GEORGIA

Demand grew among such influential westerners for some regular communication with the East. Congress responded first with a subsidy for twice-monthly runs by the San Antonio and San Diego Mail Line, dubbed "The Jackass Mail" for its use of mules. But the transportation marvel of the time turned out to be John Butterfield's Overland Mail. At its peak it had more than 250 coaches and several hundred wagons, about 2,000 employees, 1,800 horses and mules, and 240 stage stations spaced along a 2,800-mile route.

The government awarded Butterfield a $600,000-a-year federal subsidy for mail service from St. Louis to Franklin, Texas (present-day El Paso), "thence along the new road . . . to Fort Yuma . . . thence . . . to San Francisco, California, and back, twice a week in good four-horse post-coaches or spring wagons, suitable for the conveyance of passengers as well as the (Continued on page 170)

Dunes of the American Sahara

Evening settles over the Imperial Sand Dunes in southeastern California. The loose, shifting sands made this realm of desolate splendor impassable for wheeled vehicles, forcing pioneers well to the south around the most treacherous dunes. Even then many staggered out barely alive, abandoning wagons and livestock. Dead and dying animals—"almost living skeletons," wrote one man—littered the route.

Using the low afternoon sun for backlighting, a camera crew poses fashion models in Buttercup Valley, California, a few miles west of Yuma, Arizona. Movie and television companies also frequent the "American Sahara," staging combat adventures and foreign intrigues against the backdrop of the dunes.

166

Desert racers bounce over rough ground in the 300-mile Borrego Bash. Regulated by environmental agencies, this annual California event covers a prescribed

course. But uncontrolled use of off-road vehicles in the desert can scar the land and damage a fragile ecosystem that may take decades—or centuries—to recover.

safety and security of the mails. . . ." The "new road," just being started, was an improved federal wagon route for freight running from El Paso to Yuma. But instead of following it all the way, the Butterfield stages went through Apache Pass, a shortcut to Tucson.

From the outset the Butterfield kept within its schedule. Stages were late at the end of the line only three times in nearly three years. Drivers using "language that placed blasphemy as a comparative light offence" completed the first westward run in 23 days, 23 hours, 30 minutes. Remarkably, Butterfield's coaches were never attacked by Indians until the final month. It happened at Apache Pass in early 1861, when the express service was already doomed by the growing threat of southern secession. But until then, armed-to-the-teeth passengers were more endangered by rocky roads, mud holes, desert sands, and swollen streams than by Apaches. Journalist Waterman L. Ormsby of the *New York Herald* scribbled feelingly of the "heavy mail wagon whizzing and whirling over the jagged rock . . . in comparative darkness." Sleep was at first impossible, but after three days he lay down and was "quite oblivious." All was worth the excitement of pounding into Tucson enveloped in bugle calls and billows of dust, changing horses, then hurtling on toward the Pacific.

The record of the Overland Mail in maintaining its schedule is the more surprising considering the potential opposition: somewhere between 500 and 1,500 Apache fighting men roaming across southeastern Arizona, southern New Mexico, and southwestern Texas. With their guerrilla tactics the Apaches had hindered Spanish and Mexican development of the border country for 200 years. Their relentless raids on the ranchos were so effective that, by the time of the Gadsden Purchase in 1853, some areas were almost depopulated.

American newcomers at first had to contend with the same difficulties; but in 1856 a newly appointed Indian agent, Dr. Michael Steck, began regular distributions of food, dry goods, and agricultural tools. Soon he had gained the Apaches' promise that the Gila Trail stagecoaches, freight caravans, and emigrant wagons would be left alone. Except for routine thievery, the promise was fairly well kept for nearly five years. American miners and ranchers arrived in growing numbers, and U. S. troops patrolled the area.

Then one day in January 1861, the unsteady peace fell apart. Second Lt. George N. Bascom, in command of a detachment of infantry, accused Cochise of abducting a rancher's stepson and stealing some cattle. At their confrontation at Apache Pass, Cochise resisted arrest and escaped, but six of his followers were held prisoner.

Furious, Cochise and a large band unsuccessfully attacked a Butterfield stage, then seized white hostages, three from a wagon train—after tying eight others to wheels and burning them to death—and three more from the stage station. Unable to effect an exchange, the Indians killed their hostages. Lieutenant Bascom hanged the Apaches he held. And so began a dozen years of renewed warfare, merciless and mindless to the extreme on both sides.

Whites accused Apaches of "cruelties, the most vindictive revenges, and widespread injuries ever perpetrated by an American

Indian." Yet when the aging Apache leader Mangas Coloradas was taken into Army custody, he was shot dead by his guards when he forcefully complained—so witnesses said—about other soldiers' touching his feet with red-hot bayonets while he slept.

In March 1861, with Civil War clouds gathering over the United States, northern pressures to transfer stage service to a St. Louis-Salt Lake City-Sacramento route were successful, and the Butterfield operations abruptly ended. All the next year, as Union troops maneuvered to foil the Confederate invasion of the Southwest, the Apaches increased their depredations. Throughout the years of the Civil War, "Arizona was washed with blood," wrote historian John Upton Terrell. Eventually the Apaches killed or drove out most settlers and miners not living in towns.

At the war's end, national attention focused again on the frontier, beginning years of confusion and disagreement on how to deal with the Apaches. Most residents of the Southwest favored extermination. Army officers vacillated between aggressive pursuit and offers of peace treaties. Easterners and the government's Indian Bureau called for settling the Apaches on reservations. Meanwhile, small bands of hostiles raided some outlying settlement or attacked some miner, cowboy, or traveler almost every day.

In the 1870's the reservation plan won. "Apache who surrendered were to be fed and protected. Those who did not would be hunted and killed. . . ," Terrell summarizes the policy. Thousands of Indians came in to small, localized reserves.

But when others refused and continued their looting and killing, Brig. Gen. George Crook launched one of the most effective campaigns in the history of the Indian wars. In two months his highly mobile cavalry units, guided by loyal Apache scouts, repeatedly caught groups of Indians by surprise. By spring the survivors, many of them starving, were walking into the reservations by the hundred, and it appeared that the principal resistance had at last been crushed. When a year later several runaway bands resumed their pattern of theft and murder, Crook's scouts and horse soldiers sought out and whipped them again.

In 1875, as Crook was being transferred to the Great Plains to fight the Sioux, he warned against a new policy that ordered all the Apaches from their small homeland reserves to the reservation at San Carlos, north of the Gila. Members of the band led so long by Cochise, now dead, promptly vanished into Mexico. Under daring leaders, the last and most notorious of whom was Geronimo, about 150 crafty renegades began a repetitive process that continued for 11 years: They would cross the border to raid in Arizona and New Mexico, race back to the mountains of Sonora, be pursued, finally surrender, return to the reservation—and break out again.

In many cases the Apaches' complaints about reservation life were justified. Not only had they been herded from their homelands, but they had also been promised rations, goods, and farm supplies that often were never received. One Army officer declared that less than 20 percent of what was appropriated by Congress for the Indians ever reached them, and Crook—reassigned to Arizona after 1882—was frequently in conflict with "that thieving [Indian] bureau of the Interior Department."

The last time Geronimo slipped away, with only 20 followers, he raided for four months—all the while eluding 5,000 American troops who took turns guarding water holes and patrolling southern Arizona. At last a few Apache scouts and soldiers under 2nd Lt. Charles Gatewood found the band and persuaded them to surrender. On September 8, 1886, they were taken under heavy guard to the Southern Pacific station near Fort Bowie. The little remnant of one of the most amazing fighting forces the world has ever seen was put aboard a train for Florida, and Geronimo never saw Arizona again.

Near the end of the Gila Trail was a California oasis where the travelers at last divided to go their various ways. To many exhausted emigrants, the oak trees and wells of Warner's Ranch must have seemed the perpetual desert mirage turned into reality.

Kearny's dragoons billeted with the lanky Connecticut Yankee, Jonathan Trumbull Warner. In the next 30 years more than 200,000 travelers stopped to rest, resupply themselves at the store, and perhaps visit the hot, sulfurous springs beside Eagle's Nest Peak.

Today Warner's is a trading post on the highway and, just behind, a resort at the springs. In its tavern, murals of stagecoaches and fandango dancers evoke the past. The adobe building that was both stage station and Warner's home is in ruins an hour's walk away.

I sit on the porch of Warner's Hot Springs Resort, thinking back, wondering: What moment best symbolizes the transformation of that historic trail from a primitive desert track to a turnpike of the future? Was it when the railroad arrived in Yuma in 1877? Or in 1884, when Wallace Elliott's *History of Arizona Territory* counted 65 churches, 33 newspapers, and 75,000 settlers in the 20-year-old territory? Or when Army wife and frontier chronicler Martha Summerhayes, returning to Tucson in 1886, breakfasted on "iced cantaloupe . . . served by a spic-and-span waiter"?

No. My mind's eye scans back instead to Fort Bowie, to September 1886, and the vision of a man.

He stands defiant, right hand on hip, thin lips of his deep-set mouth turned down at the corners. His stocky torso is bound by a cheap, wrinkled coat; his callused feet are pinched into new cavalry boots. Dangling front and back is the long, full Apache breechcloth over white riding breeches. He is old and battered. A bullet is lodged in his right knee. Scars of other gunshot and saber wounds mark his body. His wide-brimmed hat covers a head dented by a rifle butt.

He is Geronimo, about to depart for the railroad station and the long journey to exile.

The Fourth Cavalry band serenades him. It is a brassy and ironic rendition of "Auld Lang Syne"—ironic for the old chieftain and for his longtime adversaries, yet perhaps a fitting theme song for the memories that forever will haunt the Gila Trail.

On a brisk December day, a swimsuited cowgirl and a mother and her children relax in 95-degree water piped from the hot springs nearby. Four miles from Warner's Resort, on the old wagon road, stands the adobe ranch house of John Warner—to pioneers a long-awaited oasis at the western end of the desert crossing.

North from the Platte

By Louis de la Haba

John M. Bozeman, originally a Georgian, won prominence in the West as a trail maker and entrepreneur. With mountain man John M. Jacobs he pioneered a trail between the North Platte River and the Montana goldfields in 1863. Bozeman died when only 32, reportedly slain by renegade Indians.

The cottonwoods were burning in their full autumn glory, soft afternoon sunlight shimmering through their trembling leaves. The Yellowstone flowed swiftly and noisily over its pebbly bed, "the longest free-flowing river in the lower 48 states," as my friend Warren R. McGee of Livingston, Montana, likes to remind folks from less privileged areas. We had stopped our car to look at a highway historical marker. This one, identifying the Bozeman Trail, was Warren's favorite among the 120 scattered throughout Montana.

"In the Sixties there wasn't a ranch in this country from Bismarck to Bozeman and from the Platte River to Canada," I read from the handsome, carved wooden sign. "It was land considered fit only to raise Indians and while some of the whites were hoping for a crop failure, the majority were indifferent. They didn't care how much the tribes fought amongst themselves. They were like the old timer whose wife was battling a grizzly bear. He said he never had seen a fight where he took so little interest in the outcome. . . ."

That, in a bit more than a nutshell, was how people felt about this rolling country and its inhabitants in the mid-19th century. They viewed it as a wasteland, something to be crossed as quickly as possible on the way to the comfort and riches of the Far West.

But to the Indians—especially to the Crow nation, whose home it was—the land was sacred and beautiful, an earthly paradise. Here are the words of Arapooish, a Crow chief in Washington Irving's *The Adventures of Captain Bonneville:* "The Crow country is a good country. The Great Spirit has put it exactly in the right place; while you are in it you fare well; whenever you go out of it, which ever way you travel, you fare worse."

Although the region was traditionally Crow, other Indians—notably Sioux and Cheyenne—invaded it, driven by the pressure of tribes behind them to the east, and lured by the plentiful horses of their neighbors ahead. It was generally acknowledged that this was the Indians' last, best hunting ground. A treaty signed at Fort Laramie in 1851 guaranteed Indian rights in a large area that included much of the present states of Wyoming and Montana. Although the treaty also specified the right of the United States "to establish roads, military and other posts," many of the Indians apparently thought the treaty meant white people would stay out.

For a decade they did. But after gold was discovered in southwestern Montana in 1862, a white man proposed to run wagon trains through this land from the Oregon Trail to the northern mountains. The consequences, as the shrewder of the Indians well knew, would be disastrous: Everywhere else on the plains, the coming of the whites had meant the disappearance of the buffalo herds on which the Indians depended. The threat to these last herds was intolerable.

So when John Bozeman, a gentleman-adventurer from Georgia, rode through in 1863 looking for a suitable wagon route, he barely escaped with his life. Subsequently, after a road was established against the Indians' wishes and the government sought to keep it open by force, a mean and cruel struggle resulted that dominated the early history of the trail.

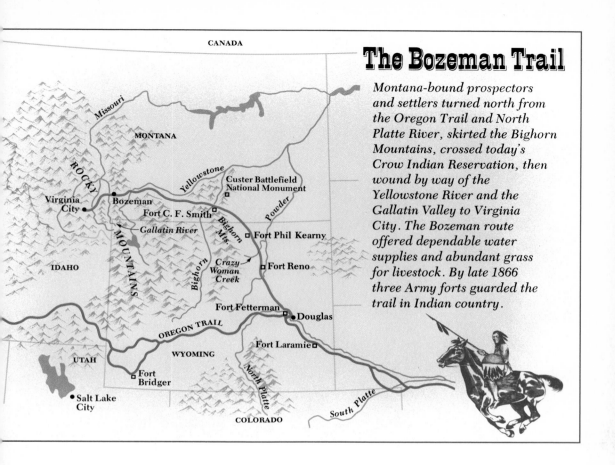

The Bozeman Trail

Montana-bound prospectors and settlers turned north from the Oregon Trail and North Platte River, skirted the Bighorn Mountains, crossed today's Crow Indian Reservation, then wound by way of the Yellowstone River and the Gallatin Valley to Virginia City. The Bozeman route offered dependable water supplies and abundant grass for livestock. By late 1866 three Army forts guarded the trail in Indian country.

The Bozeman's heyday lasted only from 1864 to 1868, when the westward progress of the Union Pacific Railroad provided a faster way to the goldfields. Nor did large numbers of settlers ever travel on the trail. Still, its story is rich and eventful. Some of the Indians' last victories against white incursions took place here; and on the Bozeman were planted the seeds of the Indians' ultimate defeat.

In 1978 I traveled over Bozeman Trail country northwest from the North Platte through empty sagebrush desert, past the pine-clad slopes and towering icy peaks of the Bighorns, west through the autumn-tinted valley of the Yellowstone, into the rich farm country of the Gallatin Valley, and beyond to Montana's bad old Virginia City. I visited the barren sites of forts from which brave men rode out at bugle's call to die. I saw places where the passage of a hundred years has not obliterated the ruts left by iron-rimmed wagon wheels. I came upon broken pieces of sheet-iron stoves made by Bridge Beach & Co. of St. Louis; nearby, rusted tin cans and spent cartridges still littered the trail. One cold, rainy evening while crossing a creek on the Crow Indian Reservation, my pickup got stuck in a gully, as many a wagon did in the old days. I was rescued and made to feel welcome by a Crow whose name was not Arapooish but Rafferty.

I saw the majesty of the Rockies at sunset as they must have loomed beckoningly ahead of avid prospectors. And in Bozeman, Montana, I heard the story of the remarkable man for whom the town and trail were named. There, too, I was entertained by the witty

Echoes of the Indian wars

Now peacefully meandering, Wyoming's Crazy Woman Creek sometimes echoed with Indian war cries and the clatter of musketry when wagon trains splashed across its shallow fords on the Bozeman Trail. Sioux and Cheyenne Indians claimed this area west of the Powder River as their hunting grounds, and grimly resisted trespassers. Despite the Indian threat, travelers often camped here before continuing another three days to Fort Philip Kearny at the base of the Bighorn Mountains. Capt. William J. Fetterman (left), a fiery Civil War veteran, believed he could "whip a thousand Indians" with a single company of soldiers. On December 21, 1866, he rode out of Phil Kearny with 80 men into an ambush that cost his life and that of everyone with him—one of the worst disasters of the Indian wars. Fort Fetterman (right), now a Wyoming state historic site where Stanley Lass works as caretaker, bears the impetuous officer's name. At far right, Mark Badgett cooks breakfast on the trail.

reminiscences of Malcolm Story, grandson of one of the trail's certifiable historical characters.

My informant on Bozeman, the man, was Dr. Merrill G. Burlingame, retired professor of history at Montana State University.

"I've always sort of admired Bozeman," he told me in his living room one sunny morning. "He was a stalwart fellow, an enterpriser. Bozeman left his family in Georgia and came west with the idea of mining gold. He was quite young, only about 25. Well, certainly he didn't find mining to his satisfaction—digging down to bedrock, up to his neck in ice-cold water, shoveling gravel by the ton.

"So he conceived the idea of scouting a trail and guiding in emigrants. Bozeman was enamored with this valley and its agricultural potential. He and his associates laid out a town here, hoping to attract people to whom they could sell land.

"He was an active man, constantly on the move. He induced some people to set up a flour mill here. He was working to establish a toll road and a ferry on the Yellowstone. He did some farming north of Main Street, and he had an interest in a little hotel. Eventually, Bozeman came to be regarded as a spokesman for this area."

John Bozeman envisioned a great migration into the Gallatin Valley, and in the spring of 1863 he left on horseback to lay out a route for the expected rush of wagon trains from the east. With him were John M. Jacobs, a veteran mountain man, and Jacobs' 11-year-old daughter by his Flathead Indian wife.

Near the mouth of the Bighorn River, they were intercepted by a band of Crow Indians. Although generally tolerant toward whites, the Crows seldom passed up a chance to steal horses or rob lonely travelers who couldn't put up a fight. Accordingly, they took the trio's horses and most of their other belongings, leaving them half naked. For good measure, they beat Jacobs' daughter with a ramrod for being in the company of white men. Near starvation, the three eventually reached help, and Bozeman went on eastward to recruit customers for his new route to the Montana goldfields.

By July 1 he had assembled a train on the North Platte River. It was made up of "forty-five wagons, mostly ox-drawn, and 90 men prepared to shoot 425 rounds without reloading," according to the recollections of James Kirkpatrick, one of the travelers.

On July 20, when the train stopped at noon near the Bighorns, a band of Sioux and Cheyennes appeared on a ridge. Spokesmen approached and told the emigrants to turn back. If they did, they would be left unharmed; if they did not, they would be killed.

Bozeman advised his companions to keep going. After all, there were 90 of them and they were well armed. But the majority decided to turn around. Determined, Bozeman and several others left the wagon train and went on to Virginia City, riding their horses at night and lying low in the daytime to avoid the Indians.

With Dr. Burlingame I went to Virginia City to see what it may have been like in the golden days, for much of the town has now been restored. Among the tawny hills we found *(Continued on page 185)*

Shifting shadows of early morning move across the Bighorn Canyon reservoir (opposite, upper photograph). Downstream the misty Bighorn River courses northeasterly through the Crow reservation, where Tribal Chairman Forest Horn (above) serves as elected leader of some 6,000 Indians. Once west of the Bighorn, travelers on the Bozeman Trail entered the country of the Crows, who tolerated the white man but hated the aggressive Sioux and Cheyenne.

ALL BY JONATHAN T. WRIGHT

Autumn on the Crow reservation

Where buffalo once roamed freely, an Indian cowboy works a herd of Hereford cattle: Tommy Half cuts out animals destined for market during fall roundup at the Mill Iron Cattle Ranch on the Crow reservation. Opposite, Alvin Morrison stands in the doorway of his cabin in the Bighorn Mountains, where he watches over the

Crow tribe's protected herd of 150 bison. At Crow Agency, Montana, schoolteacher Annie Costa helps Donovan Bull In Sight with a reading lesson in English. Most Crow youngsters are bilingual.

ALL BY JONATHAN T. WRIGHT

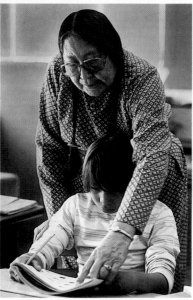

Proud and intransigent leader, Red Cloud of the Oglala Sioux symbolized resistance against whites who entered the country northwest of the Powder River. The Bozeman Trail cut through the heart of the region, and Sioux and Cheyenne warriors fought determinedly. Red Cloud did not come to terms until 1868, when the United States government agreed to abandon its military posts along the trail. The Indians usually struck from ambush, and seldom tackled a well-armed foe. Only with superior numbers and against isolated forces would they risk an open fight, as in this painting by Frederic Remington. A buckskin-clad white scout and two Indian scouts— probably Crow—fight alongside cavalry troopers firing at a fast-moving circle of mounted attackers.

rock-strewn Alder Gulch, where Bozeman labored briefly. A marker proclaims that Alder "produced over one hundred million dollars in gold." In town we paused at the opera house, now a summer theater, and at the newspaper office. On a hill nearby we looked upon the graves of five outlaws who were "launched into eternity," as a contemporary historian reported, by vigilantes on January 14, 1864.

That was just about the time that John Bozeman, undaunted by his initial failure, was leaving Virginia City to organize another party of emigrants. This time the journey was successful, and Bozeman's first wagon train arrived in the Gallatin Valley the following August. From then on, emigrant and freight trains used the trail with increasing regularity. Just as regularly, Indians attacked the travelers, running off livestock, stealing horses, ambushing stragglers, and scalping their victims.

185

PAINTINGS BY CHARLES M. RUSSELL, 1917 (BELOW) AND 1919 (ABOVE);
COURTESY THE THOMAS GILCREASE INSTITUTE OF AMERICAN HISTORY AND ART, TULSA, OKLAHOMA

"White man's buffalo!" signs one brave while his companions study the lanky longhorn with obvious misgivings. Yet Indians prized the newcomers' cattle enough to steal and eat them. Below, a Plains woman mourns her husband, whose body lies wrapped atop a promontory, his slain horse nearby beneath a ledge. To express grief, she has cut her hair and slashed her arms.

The hostilities were not limited to the Bozeman Trail but included attacks elsewhere on the northern plains against railroad construction crews, who had been working their way from the east, and on telegraph lines and mail routes. Through 1864 and 1865, attempts to deal with the Indians by force of arms were notably unsuccessful. But peace negotiations failed, too, because—though the whites did not seem to understand this—the Indians had no formally designated leaders with authority to negotiate binding agreements.

The Bozeman Trail, at least in the rugged country occupied by the Sioux, continued to be a combat zone. An account by Perry A. Burgess of a trip over the trail in 1866 includes these entries:

"August 3. . . . Passed the place where a French trader and four others were murdered a short time ago by the Indians.

"August 4. . . . a wagon had been captured by the Indians, plundered, and destroyed.

"August 7. . . . Where we nooned to-day, we saw where a man that was killed by Indians out of a train a few days ahead of us, had been buried. . . .

"August 11. . . . [tried] to find a place to ford the [Bighorn] river in vain. . . . Found graves of men that had been killed by Indians."

In 1866 the federal government decided to establish a line of forts along the Bozeman Trail. This would answer a great public clamor, especially from Montana residents, demanding protection for travelers. The military units would also—it was hoped—distract hostile Indians from the construction crews working on the advancing Union Pacific Railroad, in which the government had a heavy investment. Col. Henry B. Carrington, a desk soldier whose 18th Infantry had fought with distinction, but without him, in the Civil War, was assigned to build and garrison the forts.

Carrington and more than 700 troops arrived at Fort Laramie just as government negotiators were trying to persuade the famed Red Cloud and other Sioux leaders to permit travel through their country. When Red Cloud saw Carrington and learned of his mission, he became indignant. Pointing at the colonel, he shouted:

"You are the white eagle who has come to steal the road. The Great Father [the President] sends us presents and wants us to sell him the road, but the white chief comes with soldiers to steal it before the Indian says yes or no. I will talk with you no more."

"Some of us called *this* good logic," wrote Mrs. Margaret Carrington in her book about frontier life, *Ab-sa-ra-ka, Home of the Crows*. The comment may seem surprising, coming from the wife of an Army commander about to engage the enemy. But it illustrates the perplexity and division that existed nationwide over the treatment of the Indians on the frontier.

Many people had been horrified by such actions as the Sand Creek massacre of 1864, when nearly 200 Indians, mostly Cheyenne women and children, had been slaughtered by the Third Colorado Volunteers, a militia regiment. Pro-Indian sentiment was strongest in the East, and had the support of powerful liberal politicians and much of the press. Among most westerners and many of the military who were directly involved, the feelings were quite different. There were hawks and doves in those days, too. Mrs. Carrington, at least, perceived two sides to the question.

Before leaving for the Powder River country east of the Bighorns, Colonel Carrington wrote the first of many letters pleading for more supplies and troop reinforcements. He was particularly concerned about shortages of ammunition.

Nevertheless, the next few months were a period of intense activity. Carrington relieved the garrison at Fort Reno, a small post established on the Powder River the previous year, then moved on to the green eastern flank of the Bighorns, where he constructed Fort Philip Kearny south of present-day Sheridan, Wyoming. Later he was to send two companies 90 miles farther north where the Bighorn River comes out of the mountains, to build Fort C. F. Smith—probably the most isolated Army post of the time.

While the soldiers labored on Fort Phil Kearny, with its massive stockade of logs from the pine-wooded slopes of the mountains, the Indians almost daily attacked one or another of the work details that ventured away from the post.

"Alarms were constant," Mrs. Carrington wrote. "The ladies all came to the conclusion, no less than the officers affirmed it, that the Laramie treaty was 'Wau-nee-chee,' NO GOOD!"

I n October 1866 an exceptional and determined man named Nelson Story passed through the Bighorn country with a herd of Texas longhorn cattle. In doing so, he added another chapter to the accumulating lore of the Bozeman Trail.

I heard the tale from his grandson Malcolm, a retired rancher in Bozeman, Montana, who at 76 runs several miles each morning and still rides a horse.

Like so many others, Nelson Story went to Montana looking for gold. After three years' work he had accumulated about $40,000 worth. A businessman, not a gambler, Story knew when to quit. He went to New York City, where he converted the gold dust into greenbacks, most of which he deposited in a bank. Sewing $10,000 in cash into the lining of his overcoat, he traveled on to Texas, where he bought a thousand head of cattle. With several helpers, he drove his herd north to Wyoming.

"They picked up the Bozeman Trail," Malcolm Story related, "and when they reached Fort Phil Kearny, Carrington told grandfather, 'You can't go on up there; those Indians will kill you.' He made grandfather stop, but he wouldn't let him bring the cattle close to the fort—he wanted to save the grass there for his horses.

"So there was grandfather, camped three miles away, and he could just smell some kind of trouble. He and the others powwowed and agreed that they'd better get out of there. They left that night."

Nelson Story got the herd through and established the first cattle-grazing operation on the Yellowstone. Though the original cattle were longhorns ("leggy animals with a lot of daylight under them," my host said), good beef   *(Continued on page 201)*

Grand lady of the Bozeman, Elsa Spear Byron of Sheridan, Wyoming, has been recording the history of the trail in picture, word, and song at least since 1930. The writer-photographer's maternal grandparents moved to Wyoming over the old Bozeman route in 1881 and traded a wagon, harness, and two white mules for 160 acres near the present town of Big Horn.

PAGES 190-191:
Patterned contours reflect today's diverse agriculture—winter wheat, alfalfa, potatoes, and barley—in the fertile Gallatin Valley of southwestern Montana.

OPPOSITE: JONATHAN T. WRIGHT;
PAGES 190-191: DAVID HISER

The durable descendants of Nelson Story

Three living generations of the Story family follow in the tradition of enterprising Nelson Story, who in 1866 drove the first commercial herd of cattle into Montana over the Bozeman Trail, defying both the U.S. Army and the Sioux. His grandson, Malcolm Story, 76, lives in Bozeman, a town Nelson Story helped develop. Still active, Mr. Story runs several miles a day and helps with cattle roundups on the 18,500-acre Story ranch in the Yellowstone Valley. His son, Peter, 46 (right), owns and operates the ranch and has served as a state senator since 1973. Grandson Michael, 18, catches horses for the roundup. A representative of still another generation—Michael's son, Thomas—was born in December 1978.

193

Wildlife of the Yellowstone

In the quiet backcountry of the Yellowstone River, a wealth of wildlife lives in primeval peace. A moose dips velvet antlers as it browses on water plants. In the fog-muted dawn a cow elk and her calf roam a mountain meadow. Below, opposite, an ermine—a weasel in winter garb—peers alertly toward a strange sound. Game provided the Plains Indians more than food: Women wore dresses of elkskin. Both men and women adorned themselves with elk's teeth and tufts of ermine fur.

Restored mining town and seat of Madison County, Virginia City hugs a peaceful Montana hillside. Behind the town lies wooded Alder Gulch, site of a major gold strike in 1863. Alder Gulch soon became the target of bandits and "road agents." When law-enforcement officials proved ineffectual, citizens banded into a Vigilance Committee —vigilantes—to catch and punish criminals. Above, wooden boards mark the graves of three of the five outlaws buried on Boot Hill.

The road agent and the vigilantes

*"Reach for the sky, mister, and I'll thank you for that gold." Thus might the
notorious George Ives have spoken during the stagecoach holdup portrayed by
Olaf Carl Seltzer in the painting above. Ives took part in several such robberies in
the autumn of 1863. On December 21 of that year, a miners' court tried him
(opposite, upper painting) and sentenced him to hang. During that winter, vigilante
justice convicted and executed 21 men in Montana's gold country, including the
ringleader—Sheriff Henry Plummer! At far left, a noose hangs from a tree above
a sign attributed to vigilantes. Historians interpret the numbers "3-7-77" as a cryptic
warning to outlaws, but the actual meaning remains a mystery. At left, a mounted
posse of vigilantes returns home after a hanging.*

bulls were imported to improve the herd. The family's ranching enterprise continues today, run by Malcolm's son, Peter.

Nelson Story became one of Bozeman's leading citizens, and among his associates was John Bozeman. When Bozeman was killed in a small grassy canyon near the Yellowstone in 1867, presumably by Blackfoot Indians, Story provided the monument that marks his grave in the cemetery on a hill above the town.

Aside from its epic quality, Story's cattle drive was remarkable in that it was actually so uneventful. There apparently were only two minor skirmishes with Indians. But back in the Bighorn country Story had passed through, tragedy was brewing.

Now in their winter encampments, with plenty of buffalo jerky to see them through the bad weather, the Indians began planning new trouble for Carrington and his troops. And the colonel, intent on completing his defenses, was being ordered to take the offensive. When he did strike out at the raiders in the hills, he exposed the vulnerability of soldiers poorly trained to combat guerrilla tactics.

On December 6, 1866, Carrington just managed to escape an Indian ambush when he led troops out of Fort Phil Kearny to relieve a beleaguered wood-cutting party. One of his officers and a veteran sergeant were killed.

"From the 6th to the 19th," he wrote, "Indians appeared almost daily about the wood party or within sight of the fort."

On December 21, the wood party again came under attack, and Carrington ordered his troops out in force: 78 officers and men under Capt. William J. Fetterman. They were joined by two civilians and by Capt. Frederick H. Brown, who had orders to report to Fort Laramie but followed Fetterman, hoping to see some action and perhaps get an Indian scalp for himself.

Before Fetterman left the fort, Carrington explicitly forbade him to extend any pursuit of Indians beyond a line of hills known as Lodge Trail Ridge. That was where Carrington had nearly been killed earlier in the month. Fetterman, however, was an impatient man, contemptuous of the Indians and disdainful of Carrington for his cautious attitude. Defying the colonel's orders, he promptly led his contingent toward some Sioux decoys and beyond the fateful ridge—where perhaps 3,000 Indians lay in wait.

"The scene of action told its own story," Carrington wrote in his official report. "The road on the little ridge where the final stand took place was strewn with arrows, arrow-heads, scalp-poles, and broken shafts of spears. The arrows that were spent harmlessly from all directions show that the command was suddenly . . . surrounded. . . ."

Most of the bodies had been horribly mutilated. "Fetterman and Brown," Carrington reported, "had each a revolver shot in the left temple. As Brown always declared that he would reserve a shot for himself as a last resort, so I am convinced that these two brave men fell by the other's hand, rather than undergo . . . slow torture. . . ."

On a glittering day when the air was so clear the Bighorns seemed close enough to touch, I stood on the ridge of Massacre Hill

Creaky wooden sidewalks line Brewery Street in Nevada City, Montana. A mining camp just northwest of Virginia City, the old ghost town includes 12 of the original buildings of the 1860's as well as numerous others salvaged from elsewhere in the state. Bovey Restorations, a private organization founded in 1939, carried out the reconstruction-preservation projects in both towns. Most of the buildings contain authentic furnishings.

DAVID HISER

and looked at the scene of the Fetterman fight. With me was Elsa Spear Byron, author of several works on the Bozeman Trail and *grande dame* of Sheridan County history. Mrs. Byron was born in the shadow of the Bighorns and knows the country inch by inch. As she pointed to landmarks and described the course of the battle, I could see it unfold in its terrible detail: the unwary, overconfident soldiers cantering out of the fort; the shouted commands and bugle calls; the charge after the Indian decoys. Then, all at once, the heart-chilling appearance of thousands of war-painted Indians, whooping and howling as they rose out of gullies and emerged from wooded draws. I could almost hear the thuds of arrows, the falling bodies, flashing rifles, trampling hoofs. And then, in less than half an hour, the awful silence.

It was the worst defeat yet suffered by U. S. Army troops at the hands of Indians in the West. Not until George A. Custer's battle at the Little Bighorn in 1876 did a greater tragedy occur, a tragedy itself rooted in the conflicts of the early Bozeman Trail days.

Colonel Carrington was transferred in near-disgrace, though the disaster was hardly his fault. Ironically, Forts Phil Kearny and C. F. Smith were soon reinforced and their troops equipped with new breech-loading rifles in place of the old muzzle-loaders, as Carrington had been requesting all along.

Emboldened, the Indians continued their raiding during 1867. That year they launched two more major assaults, one at C. F. Smith and the second at Phil Kearny. Although the Indians came in force, they were repelled each time by a relatively small number of well-armed soldiers and civilians.

Still, the harassment was putting a strain on U. S. Treasury resources still depleted in the aftermath of the Civil War. It was said that the government was spending a million dollars a week to fight Indians. One cost accountant of the day, with the grisly arithmetic of war, calculated that it cost the Army $200,000 to kill an Indian. And for what? For the Bozeman Trail?

As General Sherman wrote, "That road and the posts along it had been constructed . . . for the benefit of the people of Montana, but had almost ceased to be of any practical use to them by reason of the building of the Union Pacific railroad. . . ."

And so it happened to the Bozeman, as it did to all the great western trails: The railroads rendered them of little or no use, or changed their purpose. In 1868 the posts along the Bozeman were abandoned. Fort C. F. Smith's adobe walls were left to crumble away; Fort Phil Kearny was burned down by the Indians; Fort Reno also burned, probably engulfed in a prairie fire. For the time being, at least, the Indians controlled their last, best hunting ground.

Henry Real Bird rides homeward on the Crow Indian Reservation. A former teacher, now a writer, Real Bird also breaks horses. "I just get the buck out of them and put a handle on them," he says.

Index

DAVID HISER

Chimney Rock towers over 20th-century "pioneers" retracing a section of the Oregon Trail. The clay-and-sandstone landmark rises almost 500 feet above the Nebraska prairie.

Notes on Contributing Authors

MARC SIMMONS, scholar and farrier, occupies a cluster of adobe buildings he constructed himself amid piñon and juniper trees near Cerrillos, New Mexico. His numerous writings on the Southwest include a recent collection of essays, *People of the Sun,* and the volume *New Mexico* in the special series of state histories published for the Nation's Bicentennial.

Writer and master teacher, WALLACE STEGNER for 26 years was the director of the Creative Writing Center at Stanford University. His many works of history, biography, and fiction have won him a large audience and a long list of honors, including both the Pulitzer Prize and the National Book Award. His home is in Los Altos Hills, California.

CHARLES MCCARRY, a frequent contributor to NATIONAL GEOGRAPHIC, recently completed a book recounting the dramatic adventure of the first transatlantic balloon flight, the 1978 journey of *Double Eagle II.* He is also the author of four novels, the latest of which is *The Better Angels.* He is a resident of his native Massachusetts.

Director of the University of Nevada Press, ROBERT LAXALT is also the author of half a dozen books and the university's present writer-in-residence. Like McCarry, he has contributed often to NATIONAL GEOGRAPHIC; like Simmons, he wrote one of the Bicentennial state histories (*Nevada*). Member of an old Basque family, he is former honorary French consul for Nevada.

DON DEDERA, although born in Virginia, grew up in the southwestern desert country and was once the assistant scoutmaster of a troop of Pima Indians. A former Arizona newspaper columnist, he has been for the last ten years a free-lance writer based in San Diego, California. He is the author of 11 books and many articles on subjects ranging from archaeology to oceanography.

LOUIS DE LA HABA, a former writer and editor for NATIONAL GEOGRAPHIC and now a free-lance journalist, has contributed chapters to two earlier books in the Special Publications series: *Clues to America's Past* and *Mysteries of the Ancient World.* A native of San Juan, Puerto Rico, he makes his home in Alexandria, Virginia.

Acknowledgments

The Special Publications Division is grateful to the individuals and organizations named or quoted in the text and to those listed here for their generous cooperation and assistance during the preparation of this book: Arizona-Sonora Desert Museum, Dr. Leonard J. Arrington, Dr. Davis Bitton, Jean I. Bradford, William Carpenter, Janet Carruth, Roberta Flake Clayton, Jonathan Davis, Lori Davisson, Dennis L. Ditmanson, Dr. Clifford M. Drury, John D. Ellingsen, Dr. John C. Ewers, Paul E. Ewing III, Bert M. Fireman, Suzanne Gallup, Bob Gartner, Mary Esther Gonzales, Jo Ann Graham, the Rev. Barry J. Hagan, C.S.C., Aubrey L. Haines, Archibald Hanna, Dr. Everett Harris, Scott Haskins, Ross Hopkins, Mark Junge, Alan Jutzi, James L. Kimball, Jr., Dr. Roger M. Knutson, Howard R. Lamar, Dr. Michael Malone, Robert A. Murray, Fred A. Myers, the National Park Service, Bob Ozinga, George Paloheimo, Harold Priest, Don L. Reynolds, Anne Roden, the Smithsonian Institution, Craig H. Sorenson, Don Strel, Col. William F. Strobridge, Ted E. Stutheit, Dr. Richard W. Thorington, Dan L. Thrapp, Robert M. Utley, Martha V. Wachsmuth, Lenore Woodcock Walters, James J. Weeks.

Library of Congress CIP Data

Trails West.

Bibliography: p. 207
Includes index.
   1. Trails—The West. 2. Overland journeys to the Pacific. 3. The West—Description and travel—1951-
I. National Geographic Society, Washington, D. C. Special Publications Division.
F591.T684   917.8'04'2   78-61264
ISBN 0-87044-272-4

Additional Reading

The reader may want to check the National Geographic Index for related articles, and to refer to the following books: J. B. Allen and G. M. Leonard, *The Story of the Latter-day Saints;* Jason Betzinez, *I Fought With Geronimo;* Ray Allen Billington, *The Far Western Frontier, 1830-1860;* Fawn Brodie, *No Man Knows My History: The Life of Joseph Smith;* Dee Brown, *Fort Phil Kearny: An American Saga;* J. Goldsborough Bruff, *Gold Rush;* Margaret Carrington, *Ab-sa-ra-ka: Home of the Crows; William Clayton's Journal;* Roscoe and Margaret Conkling, *The Butterfield Overland Mail;* Philip St. George Cooke, *The Conquest of New Mexico and California;* Edwin Corle, *The Gila, River of the Southwest;* Alonzo Delano, *The Far Western Frontier;* Bernard De Voto, *The Year of Decision: 1846;* Clifford M. Drury, *Marcus and Narcissa Whitman and the Opening of Old Oregon;* Robert Bruce Flanders, *Nauvoo: Kingdom on the Mississippi;* Gregory M. Franzwa, *The Oregon Trail Revisited;* Josiah Gregg, *Commerce of the Prairies;* LeRoy R. Hafen, *Handcarts to Zion;* Grace Raymond Hebard and E. A. Brininstool, *The Bozeman Trail;* Joseph Henry Jackson, *Gold Rush Album;* Dorothy M. Johnson, *The Bloody Bozeman;* David Lavender, *Westward Vision;* Susan Shelby Magoffin, *Down the Santa Fe Trail and into Mexico;* Merrill J. Mattes, *The Great Platte River Road;* Max Moorhead, *New Mexico's Royal Road: Trade and Travel on the Chihuahua Trail;* Robert A. Murray, *Military Posts in the Powder River Country of Wyoming: 1865-1894;* Francis Parkman, *The Oregon Trail;* Charles E. Shelton, *Photo Album of Yesterday's Southwest;* Wallace Stegner, *The Gathering of Zion;* George R. Stewart, *Ordeal by Hunger* and *The California Trail;* John Upton Terrell, *Apache Chronicle;* Daniel Tyler, *A Concise History of the Mormon Battalion in the Mexican War;* John D. Unruh, Jr., *The Plains Across: The Overland Emigrants and the Trans-Mississippi West, 1840-60;* Robert M. Utley, *A Clash of Cultures;* Jay J. Wagoner, *Early Arizona;* Ray B. West, *Kingdom of the Saints.*

Composition for TRAILS WEST by the National Geographic Society's Photographic Services, Carl M. Shrader, Chief; Lawrence F. Ludwig, Assistant Chief. Printed and bound by Holladay-Tyler Printing Corp., Rockville, Md. Color separations by Colorgraphics, Inc., Forestville, Md.; Graphic South, Charlotte, N.C.; National Bickford Graphics, Inc., Providence, R.I.; Progressive Color Corp., Rockville, Md.; and The J. Wm. Reed Co., Alexandria, Va.